"The sad truth is that most of the problems in the world today exist because of racism. We are all in recovery. This book provides signposts along the deep, difficult, and honest journey into a racist past that becomes unpredictable. This faithful reflection creates the opportunity to learn liberating truths and reimagine a better tomorrow. Idelette's life embodies this journey and the telling of the story invites us all into the necessary work of habitual anti-racist intentions. It lays bare the evil not only of a superiority complex but of how it in turn promotes an inferiority complex. Together these complexes rob us of both our dignity and our humanity. Rejecting white supremacy is work that we all need to do. It has humanized Idelette and relocated her in the human family as a daughter, sister, friend, and accomplice in the work of loving all God's children. I count it a privilege to have witnessed some of the steps along this precious way of love."

—**Rev. René August**, The Warehouse

"What a powerful book. With hard-won wisdom, repentance, and clear-eyed humility, Idelette takes us with her on the transformative journey of recovering racists from South Africa to Canada and beyond. One of the few white voices I trust in this space, she models repentance, truth-telling, and reparations as part of our collective work of peacemaking and liberation. Idelette is one of my greatest teachers, and I recommend her work with my whole heart."

—**Sarah Bessey**, editor of the *New York Times* bestseller *A Rhythm of Prayer* and author of *Jesus Feminist*

"Idelette Mcvicker is a trusted healer, teacher, and friend, and this book proves that she's not afraid of holding space for difficult conversations in a fiercely graceful way. This book is a beautiful, honest invitation to a better way of being human in which we embrace each other fully—I hope you'll accept it."

—⁓urtice, author of *Native: Identity,*
ʔlonging, and Rediscovering God

T0035200

"Idelette is incredibly gifted, a powerful writer and a strong leader, but the most impactful thing about her is found in this book—honesty. This is a heartbreakingly honest and gloriously transparent account of the other side of racism, the one most of us deny. Telling this story requires a person to go to the deepest places of truth, to endure the death of ego, to embrace the searing wound before applying the balm. It is the recipe for our own healing. I hope and pray that everyone everywhere will read this book because it's the kind of truth that can set us free."

—**Danielle Strickland**, communicator, advocate, and author of *Better Together*

"This book is an absolute must-read for white people seeking to be recovering racists and anti-racists. With vulnerability and intentionality, McVicker invites the reader into her story and her own journey of facing her own and her country's racism. She challenges her reader to more fully understand, embrace, and find the courage to live out the call not just to recognize the racism they've internalized but to become active anti-racists. *Recovering Racists* will encourage and liberate those who are ready to receive its wisdom."

—**Karen González**, immigration advocate and author of *The God Who Sees: Immigrants, the Bible, and the Journey to Belong*

"McVicker offers a global perspective on how racism has manifested itself in cultures and countries around the world while addressing what it means to reckon with one's own relationship with white supremacy. Her honest grappling with whiteness makes way for us all to lean in and learn from someone who has done the work to reclaim our humanity."

—**Tiffany Bluhm**, author of *Prey Tell* and cohost of the *Why Tho* podcast

RECOVERING
RACISTS

RECOVERING RACISTS

DISMANTLING WHITE SUPREMACY AND RECLAIMING OUR HUMANITY

IDELÉTTE McVICKER

BrazosPress

a division of Baker Publishing Group
Grand Rapids, Michigan

Published by Brazos Press
a division of Baker Publishing Group
PO Box 6287, Grand Rapids, MI 49516-6287
www.brazospress.com

Printed in the United States of America

Library of Congress Cataloging-in-Publication Data
Names: McVicker, Idelette, 1972– author.
Title: Recovering racists: dismantling white supremacy and reclaiming our humanity / Idelette McVicker.
Description: Grand Rapids, Michigan : Brazos Press, a division of Baker Publishing Group, [2022]
Identifiers: LCCN 2021041814 | ISBN 9781587435430 (paperback) | ISBN 9781587435614 (casebound) | ISBN 9781493435296 (pdf) | ISBN 9781493435289 (ebook)
Subjects: LCSH: Women social reformers—South Africa—Biography. | Whites—Race identity—South Africa. | South Africa—Race relations.
Classification: LCC HN49.W6 M36 2022 | DDC 303.48/4096—dc23
LC record available at https://lccn.loc.gov/2021041814

Published in association with Books & Such Literary Management, 52 Mission Circle, Suite 122, PMB 170, Santa Rosa, CA 95409-5370, www.booksandsuch.com.

Baker Publishing Group publications use paper produced from sustainable forestry practices and post-consumer waste whenever possible.

22 23 24 25 26 27 28   7 6 5 4 3 2 1

・ ・ ・ ・ ・

For those who keep longing and
working for a different world

・ ・ ・ ・ ・

One of the most difficult things is not to change society—
but to change yourself.

—Nelson Rolihlahla Mandela

The longest journey we will ever make as human beings is the
journey from the mind to the heart.

—Chief Darrel Bob of the St´át´imc Nation

CONTENTS

PART 5 REPAIR 141

FOREWORD

Sixty faith leaders from across the globe sat in a wide circle in the former minimum-security section of the apartheid-era prison called Robben Island. It was 2016, and we were there to deliberate two things: the state of People of Color in the post-colonizing world and the relationship between justice and forgiveness. We engaged these critical questions while pilgrimaging in the footsteps of Nelson Mandela on Robben Island during his eighteen years of imprisonment.

By the grace of God, our convener, Reverend René August, invited me to attend the gathering, hosted by The Warehouse, a faith-rooted community organizing group located in Cape Town. Most of the group consisted of faith leaders of Color from formerly colonized nations. White South Africans were also present.

I had never been to South Africa, though I followed the atrocity of apartheid as it reached its climax from the late 1980s through the regime's fall in 1994. The film *Cry Freedom* introduced me to the anti-apartheid struggle, while Labi Siffre's anthem "Something Inside So Strong" acquainted me with the resilience of Black South Africans. On the ferry ride to Robben Island, I had two images of white South Africans in my mind:

(1) Children and adults who were committed to upholding racialized hierarchy, and (2) the rare ones who fought it.

When I met Idelette, she intrigued me. Half of her head shaved close, the other half shaggy, bobbed, and flipped, this tallish blonde woman struck me as a curious soul with a strong core and an open heart. Her Afrikaans accent reminded me of a language I had come to associate with oppression. As it turned out, she was one of those children. Neither she nor her parents had fought apartheid. Yet she was here.

On that warm January day on the flip side of the world, Idelette leaned into our morning pilgrimage across the island for lessons and insights. By the end, we had filled the walls with scribbled reflections on large Post-it notes. Just before lunch, Reverend August asked for volunteers to take part of their lunch break to place the group's thoughts in categories to prepare for the next phase of our work.

As mealtime came to a close, volunteers filtered back into the room. I looked forward to this process but found myself surrounded by white people, with only one other Person of Color in the group—a fellow African American. Where were all the Black South Africans?

You see? The one who shapes thought shapes possibilities. The one who shapes possibilities shapes the world. Here on Robben Island, in post-apartheid South Africa, while discerning the state of Black people around the world, white people enthusiastically took over the process and were about to shape the world again.

When the group returned, all the white people were asked to leave the circle to allow safe space for the People of Color to respond to one critical question: Why did they not volunteer to help shape the group's thinking on something that will impact them so much? It was odd to create this exclusive space. Idelette left the circle. She understood the need, but a sadness washed over her. We had been all getting along so well. We were all invested in justice work across the globe. These were good white people, after all. No one wanted to make things awkward. Yet we could not ignore that the power of racial hierarchy was at play among us. We leaned into this truth and the process of addressing it.

In the end, several Black South African organizers—men and women who lead their own people every day—shared: More than twenty years after apartheid, they still struggle to believe that they, too, were created to exercise Genesis 1:26's command to have "dominion" on earth. For their whole lives and the whole lives of their parents and grandparents, they had been conditioned to follow white people's lead. It never occurred to them to become shapers of their world by helping to shape thought itself.

And when our white brothers and sisters returned they, including Idelette, listened. In the end, they had their own "aha" moments. Idelette's aha is shared within these pages.

It is a rare thing for me to stand with a book, explicitly about race and equity, that is written by a white person. Why? Because it is a rare thing to encounter a white person who has followed the lead of People of Color into their own transformation so deeply that I trust the message coming from their white body. Idelette McVicker has done the work. She has been a learner—a committed and embodied learner.

In these pages, Idelette talks of life as a pilgrimage. Through her own decades-long embodied journey, Idelette has developed a powerful voice. The stories and tears and screams and struggles of the very ones who saved her soul are the sources of her clarity and humility. Idelette says apartheid's establishing generations saw her as the realization of their dreams. "What they did not account for," she says, "was that I also needed a soul."

In the context of colonization by white supremacist imperial Rome, Brown Jesus asked, "What good is it for someone to gain the world, yet forfeit their soul?" (Mark 8:36). This question strikes at the heart of apartheid, Jim Crow, genocide, voter suppression, banning teaching about race and equity in schools, medical racism, environmental injustice, pay inequity, food deserts, and unbridled gentrification. This question strikes at the heart of it all.

They did not account for the fact that Idelette needed a soul. Idelette's recognition that she was on the verge of losing her soul powers the story and the wisdom offered within these pages.

Whiteness as a power was created by colonizing governments to determine one thing: who has the authority to exercise dominion on colonized land. Whiteness dehumanized. It deemed those pushed down to be less than human, less than image bearers, less than ones called to exercise dominion in the world. At the same time, it deemed those pushed up to be gods, possessing inherent goodness, nobility, and authority to shape truth and create the world.

We often think of struggles against white supremacy and white nationalism as isolated, disaggregated incidents of bad white people being bad. Those of us in the United States or Australia or Brazil or London might view apartheid as a distant aberration—irrelevant to life in our nation. This could not be further from the truth. Racialized hierarchy was the modus operandi of colonization. Similar political constructs of race were established across the globe by the same dominating European nations—all in relationship and conversation with each other. Thus apartheid was inspired by and aimed to perfect American Jim Crow segregation. South African "townships" were informed by American Indian removals and the establishments of reservations. It is helpful to examine the self through the framework of another's struggle. In this case, Idelette's struggle against apartheid's indoctrination is intimately tied to the indoctrination of white supremacy that has rocked the

US since the establishment of its first colonial race law in 1662 and that led thousands of white Americans to declare war on our democracy on January 6, 2021.

The work of racial healing and equity is the work of rehumanizing ourselves. It is the work of grounding ourselves in the truth that to be human is to be made in the image of God. As such, we are all called by God to steward the world (Gen. 1:26). It is also the work of grounding ourselves in the truth that while we are made in the likeness of God, we are not God. We do not possess the authority to create truth—only to reflect it. God does not authorize us to dominate our neighbors. To do so is to dominate the image of God, to enact violence against God, to declare war on God. To be re-humanized is to stand down in the fight against God for supremacy. This is the particular work of people of European descent—the descendants, benefactors, and current-day champions of their ancestors' wars against God. This is the white journey to re-humanization.

These pages reflect that journey. This book is an invitation. You are invited to take one step on this pilgrimage, whether it is your first step or one step further. You are invited to allow yourself to be simply human and to join the beloved community of humanity again.

Lisa Sharon Harper is president and founder of Freedom Road and the author of several books, including *The Very Good Gospel* and *Fortune: How Race Broke My Family and the World—and How to Repair It All.*

INTRODUCTION

This book is not a hero's journey. It is for those of us who have hit rock bottom in the human story of race. We've come to the end of our whiteness. We want to be honest about our place in the human story and heal from our internalized racism. We want to be anti-racist.[1] When I say "we," for the purposes of this book, I mean anybody who identifies as white.

Let's be clear: even as we do this work through the lens of race, race itself is a social construct and not a biological one.[2] It is a human-invented classification system.[3]

So, yes, this is a book written to white people.[4] While white people are centered as the audience, my hope is that the fruit would be "for" a larger liberation of all people, as we as white people humbly do what we need to do now. Think of this book as a moment—a side conversation—when we, as white people, gather in small groups in church basements or around tables to have a long conversation. The intention is to heal from our internalized racism so that we may do less harm. Whenever possible, I refer to the definitions and work done by Black, Indigenous, and authors of Color. Always learn from them first and foremost. Then, as we grapple with these ideas and seek out a companion for this long walk, I am here to hold space for our dismantling, our healing, and our becoming.

Ijeoma Oluo, author of *So You Want to Talk about Race*, writes, "Often, being a person of color in white-dominated society is like being in an abusive relationship with the world."[5] That means that white people—the ones who have created the white-dominated societies—are the abusers in the story of race and racism.

As a young teenager, born and raised in South Africa, I discovered that I was part of the abusive story of whiteness in our world. (As someone who has been physically assaulted, I don't say or take this lightly.) Awakening to whiteness and my participation in it shattered my understanding of who I was and where I belonged. I could not have named it as eloquently then as Oluo did. All I knew was that, growing up, I thought I belonged to a heroic story . . . until I didn't. Once I could see the role of Afrikaner people in apartheid, the legal system of racial segregation and racial oppression that lasted in South Africa for forty-six years, it became very clear I'd been on the wrong side of justice. I'd been on the wrong side of humanity. When you find yourself as an abuser in the story of race and racism, the hero narrative no longer offers a map. Instead, it felt like the hero narrative perpetuated the narratives of conquest, colonialism, domination, exceptionalism, and rugged individualism. I longed for a new way to understand my place in humanity.

I grew up in what white fascists and alt-right conservatives campaign for: a white-dominating, nationalist state. I inherited what the architects of apartheid in South Africa had hoped to protect. I was the future they had hoped to set up for success. I was the dream of their all-white future. I had everything white privilege had afforded me, including a good education.[6] All I needed to do was follow the path laid out for me. What they did not account for was that I also needed a soul.

Those apartheid laws were not just written in legal books; they harmed millions of people whose families still carry the costs. They were also written onto the land, into the air we breathed, and into my white soul. For the past thirty-plus years, I have been on a journey of dismantling that white story, the racism I breathed in and out, and the oppressive system that was originally set up to privilege me but that ultimately harmed everyone.

When the customs, beliefs, and cultures of white people operate as the standard to which other groups are compared, that is whiteness doing its work, according to the Smithsonian National Museum of African American History and Culture.[7] This is a story of naming whiteness as violence, seeing my role and place in that violence, and my longing to untangle and discontinue the legacy of that violent, internalized operating system. In *After Whiteness*, Willie James Jennings says, "My use of the term 'whiteness' does not refer to people of European descent but to a way of being in the world and seeing the world that forms cognitive and affective structures able to seduce people into its habitation and its meaning making."[8] Osheta Moore writes, "Whiteness is neither a privilege nor a blessing to be shared, it is a diseased social construct that needs to be confronted."[9]

I live and have my being in this world in a white body. This awareness was imprinted into my consciousness the minute someone wrote on my birth certificate: *blanke*/white. During apartheid, racial designations were assigned to every person in South Africa—and for many this naming by the government was itself a violence.

While my story, growing up during apartheid in South Africa, is a very particular racist story, after living on three continents I am deeply aware that racism is a pandemic.

In 2019 I took a pilgrimage through Georgia, Tennessee, and Alabama. For years I had been reading and learning about the story of race and racism in the United States, but this time I wanted to understand with my body. I longed to see, touch, taste, breathe, walk, and be with.

I visited the King Center in Atlanta with my friend Abby, walked across the street to Ebenezer Baptist Church, and listened to a recorded sermon by the Reverend Dr. Martin Luther King Jr. I drove through the Great Smoky Mountains and made my way to the 16th Street Baptist Church in Birmingham. I said the names of the four girls who had been killed there on Sunday, September 15, 1963, when four white supremacists detonated nineteen sticks of dynamite in the church.

Addie Mae Collins
Cynthia Wesley
Carole Robertson
Carol Denise McNair

I stood in silence, mindful of the violence and ideology that caused their deaths. Across the street, at the Birmingham Civil Rights Institute, I read excerpts of King's "Letter from a Birmingham Jail." I noticed how few other white people were there.

Late that Sunday afternoon, I drove into the town of Selma. Honestly, I expected a thriving tourist center to honor and commemorate the Edmund Pettus Bridge that is such a profound, global symbol in the US civil rights movement. Instead, I had to check my phone several times to make sure I was in the right place. I even had a hard time finding the plaque identifying the bridge. *Why is this bridge not a national treasure?* I wondered. It should be. It became simply another sober reminder of the work that still needs to be done.

When I walked across that bridge that Sunday afternoon, I felt ridiculous—a lone pilgrim on a bridge—with cars driving by. But I didn't care. I walked that bridge, wanting to honor the work, the strength, and the courage of those who had walked before. I am a white Afrikaner woman—a nobody in the American story—but marching across that bridge was my body's one small act of solidarity. Over the years, I have learned that it matters where we place our bodies, and part of my anti-racism journey has been to take my white body to places of pain and also to places of resistance, defiance, and liberation.

The next day I visited the Legacy Museum: From Enslavement to Mass Incarceration in Montgomery. The museum was built by the Equal Justice Initiative (founded by Bryan Stevenson) on a site where enslaved people had once been imprisoned in a warehouse. Through the brilliant work and layout of the museum, I could see how insidious racism was and is, how it shape-shifts, mutates, and takes on new forms from one century to the next, from one decade to the next. I could see how it changes to suit the white narrative and how it works to serve dominance and greed. Underneath it all, I noticed how awfully similar this evil is around the world.

That afternoon, on a scorching Monday in May, I walked through the National Memorial for Peace and Justice. This memorial, spread out on a hill in Montgomery, honors every person who suffered a racial terror lynching in the United States. I walked through the memorial twice, reading the names of victims and the names of counties where these lynchings had taken place. The memorial brought the numbers of people who suffered during this brutal time to life. It is the kind of place where you get quiet and very, very sober. This is not really a place of hope. It's a place of truth.

When I left Montgomery that night, as the sun began to set, I understood that my white story of racism in South Africa was deeply connected to the spirit of white supremacy in the United States. Because of the brutal deaths of Ahmaud Arbery, George Floyd, Breonna Taylor, and countless other people in the United States, I am more convinced than ever that white people everywhere have to get sober about our global legacy of racism, colonialism, white supremacy, whiteness, greed, and violence. We need to listen, shut up, dismantle, learn, and un-learn. We need to get racially sober.

So, why a book on race and racism by a white woman? Why not just shut up and listen?

As far as I understand, there are contradictory ideas about how white people should show up in anti-racism work. One school of thought believes that white people need to talk to other white people and call each other to account. Another school of thought believes that white people should only point to Black, Indigenous, and People of Color who are already doing the work.

Most times, white people should be quiet and only listen when the conversation is about racism. I absolutely believe we need to seek the words, wisdom, voices, and teaching of Black, Indigenous, and People of Color first. Their voices and stories need to be central in this conversation, always. In this book, I am sharing my story and my liberation journey because when I started my journey thirty years ago, I longed for the story of a white person lamenting, repenting, and wrestling with their racism as a spiritual journey.

I have been liberated by the work of Black activists and spiritual leaders in the struggle against apartheid in South Africa and by the work, prayers, and praxis of Black women from around the world. I have been liberated by Chinese women in the underground church and by a Buddhist monk in Taiwan. I have been liberated by Palestinian activists and theologians and Jewish prophets. I have been liberated by the prayers for an outpouring of the Holy Spirit in a Black church on O'ahu in Hawaii, and by the kindness of a taxi driver in Kenya. I have been liberated by Burundian farmers and Batwa mothers. I have been liberated by a Xhosa poet and a Taiwanese hair stylist. I am grateful to Indigenous leaders who have welcomed me into the circle of humanity. I have been liberated by songs, stories, education, and friendship. I am grateful to the large circle of people—from south to north and east to west—whose lives and voices reverberate with liberation. I humbly sit at their feet. May my words honor the work of so many who have liberated me. My hope is that you will find sparks for your liberation here.

Here are a few reasons I felt compelled to write this book.

In 2016 I was invited to spend time on Robben Island, a small island off the coast near Cape Town that was once used as a political prison by the apartheid government. Former president Nelson Mandela spent eighteen of the twenty-seven years he was imprisoned on Robben Island.

During that trip, our group visited the house where anti-apartheid activist Robert Sobukwe was held in silence for six years.[10] John Vorster, minister of police at the time, described Sobukwe as "a man with a magnetic personality, great organising ability, and a divine sense of mission."[11] Sobukwe had been deemed such a threat to the apartheid government that a special parliamentary decree—the Sobukwe Clause—was passed to detain him and keep him in silence. Guards were under strict orders not to speak to him.

As I sat on the cement floor, next to the single bed where Sobukwe once slept, I was overcome by the profound inhumanity of his enforced silence. I was also reminded of the power of a single voice. If our voices are that dangerous to the status quo, how dare we stay silent in the face of injustice?

A few days later, I was asked by a Black friend to take a group of writers—most of them white—back to Sobukwe's home. I felt completely unqualified, especially to lead others to the great activist's house. A voice in my head yelled, *You have no right! You are an Afrikaner woman. You are part of the people who locked Robert Sobukwe up in that house.*

Another part of me remembered the deep conviction: you dare not stay silent. So I took a deep breath. Then I asked the participants to walk in silence to the house where Sobukwe was kept. We humbly, awkwardly entered into the story, honoring and remembering the great suffering.

In 2017, on a retreat in Inanda, a township in Kwazulu-Natal, South Africa, a group and I stayed with Black host families. That night as we put on our pajamas, Jo, a white woman from Durban, turned to me and said, "You need to tell your story. You have learned things many of us are still needing to learn."

Years before, I, like Jo, would have loved to read the words of a spiritual white woman who was grappling with her internalized racism. I would have loved to see an example of someone walking this journey as part of a faith journey. I would have loved to have companions who could help me do less harm.

Just like that day when I led the group of writers to Sobukwe's home, I feel inadequate to go first in a story of becoming liberated from our internalized racism. And yet, just like that day, I also know I have been to some of these places before. And I have still not arrived. But I do believe I have learned some things along the way, so I can hold space as we journey out of the heart of whiteness and into a new way of being human. We are doing this together.

Perhaps you want to stop now and take a moment of silence too. Imagine us gathering under that tree on Robben Island, the soil beneath our feet crying out for justice. We have come to this place because we want to learn, unlearn, and dismantle. I am still awkward. I am also deeply convicted. We are here for a different world, starting with each one of us.

In September 2016, a few months after that trip to Robben Island, I listened to an interview with civil rights legend Ruby Sales. She called for a liberating theology for white people. Here's what she said:

> I don't hear anyone speaking to the forty-five-year-old person in Appalachia who is dying of a young age, who feels like they've been eradicated, because whiteness is so much smaller today

than it was yesterday. Where is the theology that redefines for them what it means to be fully human? I don't hear any of that coming out of any place today.

There's a spiritual crisis in white America. It's a crisis of meaning. . . . We talk a lot about black theologies, but I want a liberating white theology. I want a theology that speaks to Appalachia. I want a theology that begins to deepen people's understanding about their capacity to live fully human lives and to touch the goodness inside of them, rather than call upon them—the part of themselves that's not relational. Because there's nothing wrong with being European-American; that's not the problem. It's how you actualize that history and how you actualize that reality. It's almost like white people don't believe that other white people are worthy of being redeemed.

And I don't quite understand that. It must be more sexy to deal with black folk than it is to deal with white folk, if you're a white person. So as a black person, I want a theology that gives hope and meaning to people who are struggling to have meaning in a world where they no longer are as essential to whiteness as they once were.[12]

I love people. I hate whiteness. Doing this work of dismantling racism—both systemic and internalized—and leaving whiteness is a journey of liberation. The longer I've walked, the more the Spirit has nudged me to return and keep returning to white people. The burden of dismantling oppressive systems can't rest solely on Black, Indigenous, and People of Color.

Therapist and trauma specialist Resmaa Menakem says, "White folks have got to do this work themselves because white folks don't even know that we're not even speaking the same embodied language. We're not even speaking the same verbal language. We don't see the world in the same way, so we are not saying the same things."[13] White people, too, have to dismantle whiteness and every last one of its racist tentacles—in our bodies, in our minds, and in this world. We need to reclaim our humanity outside of whiteness.

I long for us to do less harm along the way.[14] "Being numb to the knife in your hand doesn't make it any less sharp," writes Cole Arthur Riley. "God, heal the wounds made in the dark."[15] Like you, I don't want our human family to suffer. I don't want to walk around with knives—not intentionally and definitely not unintentionally. I want to disarm and dismantle. I long for shalom,[16] and I am willing to do whatever it takes. Are you?

This book includes a station of liberation in each chapter. This provides a place for us to wrestle, answer questions, be honest, and go deeper with the ideas in each chapter.

As we do this work, let's remember that liberation is not a linear journey. We may move through the stations throughout the day and throughout our lives. We return to these ideas over and over again. Each time, we move a little deeper. We peel off more layers. We see new things. We unlearn a little more. We also learn new things. We make mistakes. We repair. We recalibrate. We learn to love.

My hope is that together we may heal from our internalized racism. My hope is that these pages will help correct white oppressor identities so that we may stop harming Black, Indigenous, and People of Color. My hope is to be part of healing the racialized trauma in white bodies so that we may become safe bodies in the world. My hope is that we may find our cultural identity and place in the human story and join the long lineup of good ancestors.[17]

When Paul the apostle said, "Do not conform to the patterns of this world" (Rom. 12:2), he meant the systems of the world. Systems of domination, exclusion, and hierarchy. Systems like heteropatriarchy and white supremacy. We are called out of these systems and asked to become new creations. We need to have eyes to see the ways of the kin-dom and not of the world.[18] We need to repent and turn away from the old ways and find ways to heal, recover, and become transformed. Are you ready for the journey of racial sobriety? It's time to call a meeting of the recovering racists.

Whiteness is not where our human story started, and it is not where it will end. We can be part of creating a different world. But to get there, we have work to do now.

A Note on Restitution and Repair

For this story to become a part of restitution, I cannot profit off pain and injustice. Restitution involves "seeking to set right the generational ills of inequality by engaging those who have benefited from the systems of colonialism and apartheid, directly or indirectly, in transferring wealth and social capital and reinvesting in communities that are still suffering."[19]

As a white woman talking about race and racism, I don't see my way forward without addressing money. I do this at the risk of appearing performative. My hope is that transparency, rather than performative allyship, is what remains. As we move forward, I will be referring to other examples of restitution in our conversations so we may inspire each other toward change. To that extent, 90 percent of the author income from this project will be donated to restitution in South Africa, anti-racism work in the United States, and reconciliation efforts in Canada. The other 10 percent is for the part of me that is a woman, also on a liberation journey out of patriarchy, who is finally learning that her work and her words have value.

A Note on Language

Apartheid legislation created categories of race that did not exist before the National Party came into power in South Africa in 1948. The system created racial designations that were racist and harmful and even split families. I did my best not to identify anyone by race who has not identified themselves in that way publicly. For that reason, I asked my friend Nicole Joshua to name herself in this book (see chapter 11).

I understand there are different thoughts on capitalizing racial terms. In this book, I have chosen to use lowercase for *white* and *whiteness*—not as a denial of my existence in a white body but as a posture of lament for the violence of whiteness. May our reading be a practice of lament.

I have chosen throughout this book to capitalize the words *Black*, *Indigenous*, and *People of Color*. I have also chosen to spell out this phrase, rather than use the abbreviation BIPOC because, as a white woman, I want to be mindful every time of the expansiveness, nuance, beauty, and diversity of people included in these words—from south to north and east to west in our world. As I wrote "Black, Indigenous, and People of Color," I also slowed down in my body. My best intention is not to flatten the meaning and also to acknowledge that the term itself is complicated and North American–centric.[20] As language continues to evolve, I will keep listening and adjusting accordingly. Meanwhile, as we read, would you consider joining me in being mindful and not glossing over this term? Language matters. May our reading, too, be a practice of honor.

Now, as we enter into this story and the continued work, may our bodies and our presence in this world become filled with love and liberation. May we recover from our racism.

▷ **REFLECT**

- What compelled you to pick up this book?
- At the beginning of your journey, how are you feeling?
- What do you hope to find on this journey?

PART I
WAKE UP

Practice of Liberation: Committing to Personal Transformation

"Personal transformation is a part of social transformation," writes musician and activist Andre Henry. He reminds us that we can't forget that we too have been shaped by the "toxic society we're trying to change."[1] This means that we'll also need to change.

The journey we are embarking on in this book is one of transformation. I hope we will shed old ideas, learn new ways, gain capacity, unlearn ways of being in the world, and become transformed by the renewing of our minds and our bodies. I hope this book will be part of the cocoon, part of the large container for transformation in our world.

Imagine that we, as white people, are in the caterpillar stage of comfortable whiteness. In her powerful poem "The Point. The Center. The Norm," Kimberly James highlights how white people are used to being centered, being the norm, being in a place of power.[2] Whiteness—and the status quo it's created—has been comfortable for white people. But it also set in motion the slow erosion of our humanity. It is time to move into the cocoon of transformation where we wrestle for liberation for all, as well as for our full humanity.

In his book *Falling Upward*, Richard Rohr writes, "Transformation is often more about unlearning than learning."[3] There is much for us to unlearn—greed, theft, dominance, abusive power, fear, scarcity, exceptionalism, to name a few things. But if we commit to the process, we will become transformed.

The beautiful part is that with every small act of resistance, every step toward transformation, we are also contributing to the transformation of the whole. We are not doing this work only for ourselves; we are doing this for a more whole, beautiful, and just humanity.

▷ **REFLECT**

- What kind of world would you like to live in?
- How do you want to emerge out of this process?
- What do you want to shed?
- Write a statement of commitment to your transformation or share your commitment with a recovering racist friend.

The journey of the recovering racist is a journey of transformation.

1

ACKNOWLEDGING OUR RACISM

I fervently believe that if the white person is your problem, only the white person can be your solution.

—Emmanuel Acho[1]

We live as if we are afraid acknowledging the past will tighten the chains of injustice rather than break them.

—Austin Channing Brown[2]

The person who calls himself "the least racist person in the room" is always the most racist.

—African American proverb[3]

Hi, my name is Idelette, and I am a recovering racist.
I am in recovery from the racist ideas that shaped my consciousness from the very moment I was conceived, amid one of the most racist social and political stories in history. I was born in South Africa, as an Afrikaner woman, during apartheid.

31

Apartheid literally means "separateness," and it was an intricate system of laws that separated people based on the color of their skin from 1948 to 1994. It was a political system, a human-invented system that deeply divided society. The system of apartheid and the more than three hundred years of colonized rule leading up to it robbed Black, Indigenous, and People of Color of land, resources, and education. It tried to rob people of dignity, strength, and even language.

Apartheid had done its work in such a deep way that when I left South Africa at the age of twenty-three—for work, for adventure, and to find a more loving and inclusive world—I did not have any friends who were Black, Indigenous, or People of Color.

I am now forty-eight years old. I have lived on three continents, and when I started this journey of recovering from apartheid, I believed that what we had done in South Africa was one of the worst things in the world. In fact, the General Assembly of the United Nations had labeled apartheid a crime against humanity.[4] As terrible as it was, I began learning that apartheid was not just a South African thing, or even an Afrikaner thing. I learned that the evil we needed to address, what had been around a lot longer, what took on different forms on different continents and in different periods in history, is racism.

I am in recovery from a system and a consciousness that had created a human hierarchy based on the color of someone's skin. These were all personal ideas first, which then became political ideas, which then became policies and laws, which then became embedded into structures of injustice.[5] Racist ideas also became embedded into our bodies and into our consciousness. I will most likely be in recovery for the rest of my life.

I hate racism and what it has done. I hate the pain it has caused, the structural inequality it has literally built into the land, and the economic inequality it has created and perpetuated. I hate it for the pain it causes Black, Indigenous, and

People of Color. I hate how it has killed and harmed and still kills and harms Black, Indigenous, and People of Color. I hate that we, white people, have done this. I also hate racism for how it has robbed white people of our humanity.

While I had been walking this journey out of apartheid for a long time, there was still something missing. I was running away from being called a racist, wanting to prove to the world I was not one of "those" people. Then I learned a more beautiful and liberating way: acknowledging my racism.

● ● ● ● ●

It was very early on a Friday morning in April 2016. The Reverend Kelly Brown Douglas, Episcopal priest and author of *Stand Your Ground*, stood at the podium in a room full of mostly white people in Grand Rapids, Michigan. The United States was in the throes of a presidential election campaign between the first-ever female presidential candidate and a former reality TV star. I was listening intently, furiously writing notes, when she said, "The only thing white people can ever be are recovering racists."

Thud.

Did I hear correctly? I nudged my friend Kelley next to me. She nodded.

"The only thing white people can ever be are recovering racists." As Reverend Douglas's words landed in my heart, my body simply responded "Yes." It felt like my body acknowledged the truth of it before my mind did. I came to a state of quiet acknowledgment, feeling that a long restlessness had finally ended.

I had been on a quest for years to prove to the world how not racist I was. Sitting in that room, facing the ugliest of truths about myself and my story, I finally stopped hiding. I no longer needed to hide or to prove to the world that I was a good white person. I wasn't.

I was a recovering racist.

The Bible tells us that truth sets us free,[6] although, if I am really honest, I was hoping for a different kind of truth. Not an ugly truth. Not this kind of truth.

Racial sobriety is that moment of hitting rock bottom, seeing our place in the human story clearly—no running, no hiding, no justification, no denial, no defensiveness. Only quiet, sober acknowledgment and acceptance of this very ugly truth. And right there, something else too: the beginning of liberation.

As I faced my ugliest self, I was also able to embrace my most whole self. I stopped scrambling for belonging. In that moment, I no longer had anything to prove—I couldn't. I was as human, as broken, and as beautiful as every other human being on this planet. I exhaled.

Only two years earlier, at a dinner party in our home, it was the thing I least wanted to admit. Being a racist was, for me, the most shameful thing I could ever be accused of. When somebody said the word *racist* at the table, jokingly indicting me and a handful of other white people at the table, I burst into tears. I was as fragile as white could be.[7] The word *racist* carried deep shame for me because it was interconnected with my culture, my identity, and the story of my people. I felt like I had something to prove to the world.

I was born in South Africa in 1972, on the white side of the hospital. October is already spring in South Africa, but my mom says that day was so cold and miserable that she had to buy a new winter robe for her hospital stay. It was a cold and miserable season in the history of South Africa.

In 1948 the National Party, an ethnic, nationalist party that promoted Afrikaner interests in South Africa, gained political power and won elections based on their policy of racial segregation. Only white people had voting rights at that time, and after winning, the National Party began implementing a comprehensive set of laws to segregate people based on race.

Afrikaner people made up only about 5 percent of South Africa's population, and apartheid was how a white-minority government dealt with its presence in a majority Black country.

I was unaware of this political drama when I was born, and for the most part I grew up in a white bubble. Apartheid had achieved exactly what it had set out to do: separate people. It had created a "whites only" story for any white person who wanted to cling to that. I grew up steeped in Afrikaner nationalism, Afrikaner symbolism, and Afrikaner history. I was raised to be proud of Afrikaner culture and accomplishments.

Perhaps it would help to clarify that there are two quite distinct cultural groups of white people in South Africa—those who are white and speak English and those who are white and speak Afrikaans. Only white South Africans who speak Afrikaans are called Afrikaners. Afrikaans, my mother tongue, is a Creole language consisting of Dutch mixed with Malay, Portuguese, Indonesian, and the Indigenous Khoekhoe and San languages.[8] In spite of its rich and diverse origin story, Afrikaans was implemented as a weapon to strengthen Afrikaner nationalism.

For the first eighteen years of my life, I grew up in an almost exclusively white, Afrikaans-speaking environment. Our house was in an all-white neighborhood. For twelve years of my life, I went to an all-white school with all instruction in Afrikaans (other than for our English classes, of course). Every Sunday we sat in an all-white, Afrikaans-speaking church. These white environments had been intentionally created by the racist laws of apartheid. My personhood was formed in one of the most extreme racist political systems in history.

In some sense, I had been not to the mountaintop of humanity but to the bleakest valley of whiteness. I imagine that the creators of apartheid had intended for me, as a daughter of apartheid, to reap only its privileges and its benefits. But how can you commit—and benefit from—a crime against humanity and not bear its weight?

Years later, sitting in that cold lecture hall in Grand Rapids, I was still struggling for clarity, healing, and freedom from what I had learned and internalized during those first decades of my life. I was looking for any and every crumb of liberation in order to reclaim and recalibrate my humanity. I wanted to make the world better. I wanted to pay for that crime against humanity. I didn't know how, but I was desperate to find a way. I knew I was not responsible for all of it, but I was responsible for my part.

"I am a recovering racist," I told Kelley later that evening. It was the first time I had said those words out loud, and it felt important to do so.

She nodded. She knew.

● ● ● ● ●

It wasn't God who created race. People did. In 2000, scientists finally proved that race is a social construct, never a scientific or biological one.[9] J. Craig Venter, the American biotechnologist who led the research team at Celera Genomics Corporation, reported, "We all evolved in the last 100,000 years from the same small number of tribes that migrated out of Africa and colonized the world."[10] As human beings, we share 99.9 percent of our DNA. "The differences that we see in skin color do not translate into widespread biological differences that are unique to groups," explained Aravinda Chakravarti, a geneticist at Case Western University in Cleveland.[11]

Black authors, Indigenous authors, and other authors of Color have contributed—and are contributing—numerous works on the history, impact, intricacies, and complexities of race and racism. We start there, always. It is difficult for those of us who have constructed societies based on a hierarchy of race and value, and who have perpetuated that racism, to perceive racism as clearly as those who have lived with it, have been forced to "dance" with it, and have been at its mercy.

In *Between the World and Me*, Ta-Nehisi Coates powerfully points out that race did not create racism. Rather, racism gave birth to race. "Americans believe in the reality of 'race' as a defined, indubitable feature of the natural world," he writes. "Racism—the need to ascribe bone-deep features to people and then humiliate, reduce, and destroy them—inevitably falls from this inalterable condition. But race is the child of racism, not the father. And the process of naming 'the people' has never been a matter of genealogy and physiognomy so much as one of hierarchy."[12]

Caste: The Origins of Our Discontents, Isabel Wilkerson's extensive research into the infrastructure of racism, brings more clarity. "Caste is the infrastructure of our divisions," Wilkerson writes. "It is the architecture of human hierarchy, the subconscious code of instructions for maintaining, in our case, a four-hundred-year-old social order."[13]

In *How to Be an Antiracist*, Ibram X. Kendi reminds us that racism is both systemic and a disease. He writes, "I thought of racism as an inanimate, invisible, immortal system, not as a living, recognizable, mortal disease of cancer cells that we could identify and treat and kill." He adds, "Racism has always been terminal and curable. Racism has always been recognizable and mortal."[14]

The vile serpent of racism lives in systems, in structures, in bodies, in hearts, and, if we let it, in the spaces between us.

* * * * *

My racism is not the kind of racism that wears a hood, calls names, or storms a capitol building. No, it has been much more subtle, but certainly not benign. The disease of racism that settled into my body is that of seeing the world through a false narrative of race, defining our humanity by a hierarchy of value and worth.

If you'd asked me when I was growing up in South Africa whether I was a racist, I would have said, "No way!" I spoke up against racist jokes at backyard *braais* (South African BBQs) and thought racist people were small-minded and unsophisticated. I certainly did not identify with the label. But years later, nearly a decade after apartheid had ended in South Africa, I felt like I was still carrying apartheid in my body. I felt chained down by a soul heaviness—something I had trouble naming. I could not shake the idea that my liberation had not come yet; that there was still work to do, connected to the pain and oppression we'd caused Black, Indigenous, and People of Color in South Africa.

"In America, nearly all of us, regardless of our background or skin color, carry trauma in our bodies around the myth of race," writes Resmaa Menakem. "We typically think of trauma as the result of a specific and deeply painful event, such as a serious accident, . . . but trauma can also be the body's response to a long sequence of smaller wounds."[15] Trauma research specialist Bessel van der Kolk writes that traumatic experiences "leave traces on our minds and emotions, on our capacity for joy and intimacy, and even on our biology and immune systems. Trauma affects not only those who are directly exposed to it, but also on those around them."[16] I did not have language for it then, but I sensed that I was carrying apartheid in my body— the weight of the oppressor.

James Baldwin writes, "We carry our history. We are our history."[17] I wondered if the same were true for oppressors. Then one day while my kids were still babies, I sat down at my computer and wrote, "I have apartheid." I wasn't just wrestling with a system out there; I felt it inside me. I wrote:

I am sick, but I don't have the kind of disease a doctor could ever diagnose. Only history books could tell you what I have.

I have apartheid.

It's a struggle of the soul. It's an inflammation of the heart. It's the cancer that lives in the walls between us. I have separation in my bones, division in my blood, fragmentation in my soul.

It's a human condition. It's a learned condition. It's a condition of the heart.

I heard echoes of this idea years later when Wilkerson wrote that caste "embeds into our bones."[18] My soul was a witness.

The day I recognized apartheid—along with its internalized racism—as a disease in me and in our world and not just something that happened in the past was the day I began finding medicine for the journey. There is not one prescription for all white people. We need to figure out our own way back to our humanity. And we need to take responsibility for our own recovery journey. Hopefully, as you read this book, and especially the many books by Black authors, Indigenous authors, and other authors of Color, you will create your own treatment plan and be encouraged to keep going.

A racist is someone who has contracted the disease of racism—seeing the world through a hierarchy of worth based on skin color—and who allows and benefits from the systemic abuse of power, either consciously or unconsciously. To be in recovery from racism is to acknowledge our internalized bias and prejudice while embracing a daily treatment plan to uproot and kill the disease, both within the body and in our world.

"Recovering" is something we do after we've failed. The systems of hierarchy created by white people over the centuries have failed humanity. But when we have failed, we can also recover. Yes, we can hide in the corner, numb, or hide in white enclaves. Or we can face the ugliness, pick up the pieces, and do whatever it takes to make things right. That is the brave—and right—thing to do.

"Recovering" is also what we do after we get sick. White people have been diagnosed with the disease of racism, and this is our journey of recovery. We need to get rid of the disease, remove the toxins from our bodies and our world, and work on recovering.

"You are racist, love, but it's okay to admit it," says Marley K. "I'm ready for you to admit it so that we can move on to bigger things. You denying the obvious stalls the long road to healing. Take a moment to sit with this new/old revelation. Your racism is a product of nurturing and nature. Own it."[19]

It's time to own and acknowledge our racism.

Station of Acknowledging

Recovering from racism is not linear. It is much more like finding ourselves in the giant circle of humanity. Within the circle, we make decisions about how we respond to the challenges and the wounds of the journey, as well as to our fellow travelers. When we begin to heal and unclench, we move closer to the center, which is love. As we learn and unlearn, we also move closer to love. Some days we move through all the stations in one day. Other times we can hang out at a station for months, doing the deep, inner work required there. We come to this journey with our own unique stories and personalities. I don't know where your journey will take you; my best hope is that it will lead you to love.

We can't heal or make right what we don't acknowledge. That is why we start here. *Acknowledge* means "to accept or admit that something exists, is true, or is real."[20] It is here where we stand in the ugly truth that we have been a part of committing sins against humanity. We may not personally be responsible, but when the community we have been a part of or were raised in has committed injustice against a whole group of people, we, as individuals, need to take up our responsibility for the collective harm that was done. We cannot sweep it under the rug.

Acknowledgment is the opposite of denial. It is the opposite of hiding. It is the opposite of coming up with defensive arguments to prove that we are not like that or that we do not belong to "those people." This is the history we need to own.

40

Take a deep breath.

It's okay. This is the work of liberation and transformation. As we do our work, walk our journey of recovery, and join the movement to rid our world of racism, we can join in creating a different world.

This is not where the story ends. We start with acknowledgment.

▷ REFLECT

- As you reflect on the ideas and stories in this chapter, what do you notice rising in you?
- What do you need to acknowledge at this time? Is there something you need to admit to yourself and others?
- How have you, or your ancestors, been part of failing humanity? (This is not to shame. This is simply to take an honest account. If shame rises for you, share it with someone. We will also address shame in chapter 5.)
- What is your responsibility (meaning your ability to re-spond) to the past?
- Have you ever acknowledged out loud to a trusted friend that you are a recovering racist? (Remember, this is only to be shared with someone who is also a recover-ing racist; it is not to create more harm.)
- What does it mean to you when you say you are a recov-ering racist?
- Where have you noticed an apartheid in your world or in the world?

The journey of the recovering racist starts
with acknowledging our racism.

2

AWAKENING

> The most painful act the human being can perform, the act that he dreads the most is the act of seeing. It is in that act of seeing that love is born, or rather more accurately, that act of seeing is Love.
>
> —Anthony de Mello[1]

I originally wanted to start this conversation by telling you how I am possibly the worst white woman in the room. I used to think that gave me the right to tell my story. Now I know it's simply another way internalized white supremacy wanted to show up. White supremacy thinking gave me only two options: best or worst, winner or loser. If I couldn't be the best white woman, I had to be the worst white woman. Now I am learning I have another option: human.

So, here I am, showing up for the first meeting of the recovering racists. I am not any more special than anybody else in this room. I am not any worse either. I am simply here for the work, learning and unlearning alongside you.

● ● ● ● ●

I was sixteen the first time I witnessed the world's darkness. It was June 1988. My dad, who was also my German teacher, was leading our tour group of rambunctious teenagers through the gates of Dachau, a concentration camp outside Hamburg, Germany. The imposing black-iron entrance was etched with the words "Arbeit Macht Frei" ("Work sets you free"). It was a summer's day, but what I remember about that day was how gray it was and how cold. Coldness rose from the ground and went right into my skin. I remember the starkness, like I needed a cozy blanket or something soft, but there was nothing soft to touch. There was no comfort in that place. The gravel crunched underneath our feet. A great silence fell over all of us, and nobody needed to tell us to be quiet.

South Africa had its own history of concentration camps during the Anglo-Boer War that raged from 1899 to 1902 between the Afrikaners and the British. I learned about the white camps, but there had also been separate Black camps. Officially, over fourteen thousand Black people died in those concentration camps, while recent research suggests at least twenty thousand Black deaths.[2] In the white camps, more than twenty thousand children and four thousand Afrikaner women died, either from starvation or disease.[3]

But until we walked through those gates at Dachau, the evil of the world still felt very far away from my preoccupation with school, boys, and sports. I hadn't yet connected how trauma had been a birthplace for a frenzied nationalism in the consciousness of my own people.

I have a faint memory of that day: being in a basement room. It looked like a bathroom. It took me a while before I realized what the rows of shower heads meant. Until I stood there in the gas chambers and saw how there was no way out once the door was locked, until I saw those shower heads with my own eyes, I hadn't entered the story. Then I noticed the photos on the shower walls. It took my mind some time to register what I was seeing: human bodies, naked and piled on top of each other.

Once I saw the bodies, I could not unsee them.

● ● ● ● ●

A few months later, I walked into the Paarl Library, located in a beautiful old home built in the Cape Dutch style with thick white walls and wood shutters. Growing up, I was an avid reader and went to that library at least once a week. I'd read my way through the children's library—first the Afrikaans side and later the English side.

That day I turned the brass knob on the large wooden door and walked into the quiet space. I passed the long wooden counter on the left with librarians checking out books and said a quiet and polite hello. Then I walked toward the books on turnstiles, with special themes, where I always made my first stop.

I noticed a sign that read "Recently Unbanned Books."

I leaned in a little closer. I'd vaguely understood that books had been banned—basically any book that criticized the apartheid government. What had made them so threatening before? I picked up a book and looked at the title and the cover. Nothing suspicious. What's a banned book supposed to look like?

As I looked through the books, feeling a little defiant, my eye caught the title of an André P. Brink novel: *A Dry White Season*. Brink was a renowned Afrikaans writer. The book seemed innocuous enough. I was both curious and naive. Over the next few days, I was invited into the story of a friendship between a Black custodian and an Afrikaner teacher. I had never seen a friendship lived out between a Black man and a white man on equal grounds. I was hearing a telling of the apartheid story I'd not heard before. I was also catching a vision of our human story—as equals.

As I sat on my bed and read, I walked through a door inside my mind. I entered into a world much more brutal than the government-controlled Afrikaner story I'd known—a world of police violence, oppression, racism, and senseless murder. There was another frightening dissonance rising: the Afrikaners were not the good people in this story.

A spotlight was pointed at a part of the world that existed but that I'd never before seen. I'd heard rumors of this reality. The voices of anti-apartheid activists suddenly rang out more clearly, lining up with the version of the world I was reading about. My eyes were opening, and slowly, slowly, I was adjusting to the light of this new reality.

Meanwhile, this full and ugly truth swung like a demolition ball at everything I had once believed to be true. My understanding of the world and what it meant to be human had been like a house. Brick by brick that house was being demolished: my worldview, my identity, my faith, my trust in authority, my sense of belonging, and my belief that Afrikaner people were the good people in the story.

Once I closed that book, I found myself standing in a giant pile of rubble in an empty lot. My inner person looked around and saw that the world as I knew it had crumbled. I turned around and walked off into the world. I'd caught a glimpse of what it could look like to be human. But I didn't know where to find an expansive view of love, belonging, and being human. I didn't know then that I was looking for an environment of dignity, respect, and a sense of deep connectedness to other human beings, to all of life. I was looking for love at the core of every decision and every interaction. And I knew that the people and institutions who had created the world I grew up in didn't have the answers.

I had seen the ugly truth inside my own country. It was my first awakening.

●　●　●　●　●

I've heard that the three things that most influence our lives are the books we read, the people we meet, and the places we see.

These all offer doorways and windows into new ways of seeing and understanding. Dachau opened my eyes to the evil in our world. *A Dry White Season* opened my eyes to the truth about apartheid in South Africa. But if you asked me who most influenced me growing up, it wouldn't be one person but all the people I never got to do life with. The Black friends I never met. The neighbors of Color we never had. Looking back, I see that it was the *lack* of these relationships that most profoundly marked me.

Many white people in the United States and around the world had an awakening to the reality of racism after the brutal death of George Floyd on May 25, 2020. Those eight minutes and forty-six seconds that Derek Chauvin had his knee on Mr. Floyd's neck, ultimately leading to his death, shook the world. The challenge is not to rely on our first awakening but to keep waking up. My first awakening happened over thirty years ago—and I still have to come to this work every day. In fact, I long to wake up a little more every day.

The lenses with which I see the world often prevent me from seeing the full story. I don't see what I don't see unless I lean in to what those most affected are saying. But every time the light is turned on, I am also liberated. Every time I awaken a little more, there's the possibility of doing less harm. Awakening requires consistently listening to different voices, seeing from new perspectives, going to new places, shifting my point of view, and learning from others.

Awakening is liberation. Awakening is recovering from our racism. But from that very first awakening to now, the story of recovering from my racism has not been a rush of liberation. It's been more like a repetitive, humbling *thud*.

Station of Awakening

Choose an object or image that represents awakening to you. It could be something like a window, a door, a lightbulb, or the sun. Choose something that feels authentic to you. Whenever you see this object or image, let it remind you to lean in to your awakening.

▷ REFLECT

- Who or what first awakened you to racism in the world?
- What wakes you up?
- Who has helped shift your perspective?
- What do you need to do to pursue awakening?

Dear God,

What am I not perceiving? Who is missing? Whose stories do I need to listen to? We have prayed so often, "Open the eyes of my heart, Lord." I pray now: Open the eyes of white people's hearts, including mine, to see the realities of racism in our world. Open our eyes to see our place in the story.

The journey of the recovering racist is a journey of awakening.

PART 2
LEAVE

Practice of Liberation: Committing to the Long Walk

This is a long walk.[1]

Apartheid in South Africa officially lasted forty-six years. From 1948 to 1994, millions of Black, Indigenous, and People of Color were oppressed, dehumanized, killed, jailed, silenced, and denied basic human rights and dignity. Consider also the more than three hundred years of colonization leading up to apartheid.

Institutionalized slavery in the United States lasted 246 years. After the transatlantic slave trade and domestic slave trade in the United States ended, the Jim Crow era lasted another hundred-plus years, until 1968.

In Canada, residential schools for Indigenous children existed for more than a hundred years, with over 150,000 Inuit, Métis, and First Nations children attending these schools. The generational impact of these schools lingers.

Democracy in South Africa has existed, at the time of the publication of this book, for less than three decades. Residential schools in Canada have been closed for less than thirty years. A new Jim Crow era is continuing through the prison system in the United States, and Black life still does not matter the way it needs to.

These have been very long years of oppression, injustice, trauma, and pain. How dare we, as white people, want Black, Indigenous, and People of Color to "get over" these centuries of oppression? How dare we want to snap our fingers and tell any Black, Indigenous, or Person of Color to "move on" or "let the past be the past"?

It is much more comfortable to "arrive" at some kind of idyllic destination of racial unity and reconciliation. But justice and liberation have not been worked out in the souls of most white people. We don't yet have the inner muscles for that different kind of world. We don't get to stay in white fragility;[2] we need to build our capacity for this work. There are operating systems to dismantle and new ways of being to learn. We have to unlearn dominance, triumphalism, exceptionalism, and hierarchy—to name only a few things.

It took the Israelites forty years of wandering in the desert to unlearn the ways of Egypt. Those forty years represent the time it took for a new generation to arise (Num. 32:13). A different world is possible, but we are not there yet. Creating a world without racism, in which every person is treated with love, dignity and respect will take time. Are we willing to commit for the long run?

ALLY ANTHEM

As I begin the work
and embark on this season of change—
I am allowed to feel anxious
I am allowed to feel afraid
I am allowed to feel exposed.
Despite this—
I will not weaponize my tears
I will not play the victim

I will not expect black women to fix me
I will never question the validity of the cause
When I want to quit—
I will dig deeper and meet with my ugly
I will remember my discomfort is nothing compared to the
    violence
my privilege had inflicted.
I will remind myself on the side of history I wish to belong.
I must be aware—
That I will lose friends, positions and parts of myself
That this work will be my unraveling
Today I declare I am committed to this work,
to break the soul ties with my privilege and
proclaim a true and authentic allyship for
the first time in my life.[3]

Take a large bowl or bucket to represent the time period you want to reflect on—for example, 246 years of institutionalized slavery in the United States, 46 years of apartheid in South Africa, over 100 years of Indigenous children suffering in the residential school system in Canada, or centuries of racism in our world.[4]

Find a water source and slowly, very intentionally fill the large bowl or bucket. As you let the water fill the container, reflect on the period of oppression you are holding in your mind. What was that period of time filled with?

Put the bowl or bucket in a place where you can be mindful of it throughout the day. At the end of the day, slowly empty the container, giving thanks for any new insights or awakening. Be mindful of how long it takes to empty the container.

What are you noticing?
What thoughts are coming to mind?
What are you feeling in your body?
What is required of you?

Let's be clear: as white people, we can never truly understand what racism is or how it has affected Black, Indigenous, or People of Color. This exercise does not make anyone an expert in the suffering experienced by people who have been oppressed. This is simply an exercise to help us become more mindful and to gain a little more understanding of how very *long* these periods of oppression have been.

Share your thoughts in a journal or with someone who is also on this journey of recovering from racism.

▷ REFLECT

- Take some time to reflect on Vean Ima Torto's "Ally Anthem." Which ideas or words stand out to you?
- What does it mean to you to meet with your "ugly"?
- What violence has your privilege inflicted? Can you name it?
- What does committing to the long walk mean to you?
- What are you leaving behind?
- Write out a statement of commitment to this long walk or share your commitment with a fellow recovering racist.

The journey of the recovering racist is
a commitment to the long walk.

3

IMAGINING A
DIFFERENT WORLD

A new world is possible. It doesn't have to be this way.

—Andre Henry[1]

Prophets are dangerous. But dangerous to the status quo.
Prophets are God-intoxicated people. And they are dangerous to people intoxicated by the status quo. Prophets
are intoxicated and caught up in God's dream of a just and
loving world.

—Anthony Smith[2]

We are not made for resignation, but for freedom.

—Steven Charleston[3]

Freedom! Oh, freedom! Oh, freedom, freedom is coming.
Oh, yes, I know.

It was 1997 and I was a young journalist in the city of Taipei. Outside the air was hot and sticky, but inside the auditorium I was invited to catch a glimpse of a different world. Fifty Youth Ambassadors—young representatives from fifty nations—marched down the aisles belting out these words of freedom. They were called the World Vision Youth Ambassadors.

This was one of my favorite stories to cover for the *China Post*, the English-language daily newspaper I worked for as community editor in Taiwan. The Youth Ambassadors were an initiative of Jerry Chang, the visionary executive director of World Vision Taiwan at the time. Chang had been an engineer who had used his knowledge of building bridges in the United States to become a bridge builder of a different kind in Taiwan.

The World Vision Youth Ambassadors program was as ambitious as it was glorious. Imagine for a moment fifty young people, each dressed to represent their cultural identity, singing songs of peace, love, and justice in different languages together. It moved me to tears every time I watched a performance. They didn't just sing together. They also studied principles of peace and nonviolence and learned to walk out these principles on the bus or in the dormitory—a bunch of teenagers who were learning to live together as a microcosm of our human family. There, in an air-conditioned bus, students from nations that had been at war sat next to each other, learning what it meant to be human together. Students who previously had been sponsored children sat next to students who had grown up wealthy. Indigenous Youth Ambassadors sat next to representatives from nations that had colonized.

The choir—a tangible, visual representation of the nations of the world—gripped my imagination. That song, too—of freedom being on its way toward us—caught hold of my heart. In many ways, I had already seen freedom come to a nation.

In 1994, only a few years earlier, I had voted in my very first election. I had joined twenty-two million other South Africans who showed up at booths all across the country to vote in our first free and fair democratic election. For most of the people who voted that day, it was their first time. Not because they were finally of voting age, like me, but because until that day, April 27, 1994, only white South Africans had been allowed to vote. Desmond Tutu was sixty-two when he voted that day. He was a Nobel Peace Prize recipient and the archbishop of Cape Town. He was revered and respected around the world. But in South Africa, that day was the first time he got to exercise his civil right to vote.

"How do you describe falling in love?" he responded when asked how it had felt voting in that election.[4] "It was giddy stuff," he wrote in *No Future without Forgiveness*. "The sky looked blue and more beautiful. I saw the people in a new light. They were beautiful, they were transfigured. I too was transfigured. It was dream-like."[5]

In 1994 I was an idealistic journalism student living in Grahamstown in the Eastern Cape, and I understood that we were a part of world history. It was a day that would become as historic as the day Nelson Mandela was released in 1990 and the day the Berlin Wall fell in 1991. The world was changing at a rapid pace, and it was exhilarating to be a part of it.

Until that day in 1994, the National Party had ruled with an iron fist. Forty-six years of white minority rule in a majority Black country. "The only way to keep an entire group of sentient beings in an artificially fixed place, beneath all others and beneath their own talents," writes Isabel Wilkerson, "is with violence and terror, psychological and physical, to pre-empt resistance before it can be imagined."[6] As a nation, we had certainly seen and experienced that violence and terror. A few years later, during the Truth and Reconciliation Commission hearings, we would begin to hear the details of some of that violence, especially on the part of the apartheid government, who had kept their activity concealed and always slanted favorably.

But on that Wednesday, I walked toward the election station, astounded at the number of people who had shown up to vote. I fell in line, ready to wait. I can still feel the sun on my face. I remember Black women in front of me singing and *toyi-toying*, a dance that had become synonymous with the struggle for freedom and justice. Joy was radiating from their bodies and through their voices. But it was more than that. It felt like joy was radiating from the heavens, down on us, and joy was radiating up from the earth. I don't remember voting, but I remember that moment. It felt like everything was absolutely and completely right with the world. Justice was finally coming, and so peace, too, was present.

I have heard some define *peace* as "nothing broken, nothing missing." On that day, it felt like our broken system was finally being set right and, politically, no person was intentionally excluded from the story.

I felt so proud to be a South African that day. I celebrated the end of apartheid along with millions of people lining up for miles to vote all across the country. I tasted justice and peace, and that memory—that very visceral awareness of the world feeling gloriously right—would carry me when everything did not feel right in my body and my soul, when I had to begin grappling with the truth of apartheid and what it meant to be an Afrikaner woman in the world.

From this experience, I know now what justice feels like in my body, and I know what it is meant to look like for *all* people. It is not just an esoteric concept on the pages of the Bible or in the mouths of those calling for it. It lives in laws and in the movement of bodies, and it lives in the spaces between us. When justice comes, the rocks proclaim God's glory and the sun rises with healing in its wings (Luke 19:40; Mal. 4:2).

It was on election day—a day from then on celebrated as Freedom Day—that I caught a glimpse of true and beautiful liberation. I caught a glimpse of what could be.

For many, political freedom came on that day. For me, in so many ways, liberation was just beginning. I long for that sense of freedom in our world, not just for some but for everyone. I long for a different world to come into being. Holding on to that vision makes my bones strong and my feet firm. It is sustenance for when the journey gets long. I've caught a glimpse, and until freedom for everyone comes, I will keep holding on, holding out, and doing my part for that different world.

Station of Imagining

It's all right to talk about the new Jerusalem, but one day, God's preacher must talk about the new New York, the new Atlanta, the new Philadelphia, the new Los Angeles, the new Memphis, Tennessee. This is what we have to do.

—Martin Luther King Jr.[7]

The Bible calls us to a prophetic kind of seeing—to open the eyes of our hearts so that we may see things as they are and as they could be. (Think about Elisha's prayer in 2 Kings 6:17.) Prophetic seeing is not just for some day when the future we hope for finally arrives. It's also for naming the status quo for what it is, seeing it not with rose-colored glasses or white lenses but with its pain and injustice, cruelty and horror. We remember the words in Isaiah 35:6 that even in the wilderness, water will gush forth. When everything seems dry and hopeless, like a desert land, the Spirit of God can create "streams in the desert."

Write or say a prayer to express your longing for this new world. Find a song or a poem that represents the idea of freedom to you, not just individual freedom but collective liberation.

▷ REFLECT

- When or where have you caught a glimpse of the new world that is possible?
- Where do you feel freedom in your body? Do you? Find a way to express the concept of freedom in your own body. Be mindful of any resistance. Where does that come from? Journal about it or talk to a recovering racist friend.

The journey of the recovering racist is a journey toward a different world.

4

GETTING COMFORTABLE
WITH DISCOMFORT

You are at the beginning of something new.
You are learning a new way of being.

—International Council of
13 Indigenous Grandmothers[1]

In June 1995, I got on a plane and flew to Taiwan. It was the year after the first democratic election in South Africa and six months after I had graduated from journalism school. My boyfriend and I planned to teach English.

I was chasing after something. I only knew to name it freedom. It was not a bombastic, individualistic freedom that disregarded the well-being of others but rather an intrinsic freedom that connected me to everyone and everything else.

I had an inkling of a world that echoed with this freedom. I could sometimes feel it in the air around me. That freedom beckoned to me, singing songs of a different way of being human. It lived in the spaces between words in books and in the way the Drakenstein Mountains stood behind our house in Paarl at dusk. It lived in the waves of the Atlantic Ocean, crashing onto the rocks in Sandbaai. It was an itch, an intuition, a compelling—a different kind of knowing. It was a cry that rose through the soil and a voice in the wind and the waves that kept calling me out into a much larger world.

I was so hungry for that world. I wanted to leave the smallness I felt within and without. I wanted to bust through, but I didn't know how. All I knew was that I had to leave that old world behind.

On the night we landed in Taiwan, we took an airport bus into downtown Taipei to catch a yellow taxi to Tienmou. We were chatting, standing on the sidewalk in a brand-new city, when I suddenly heard a low buzz. The sound grew louder and louder—like a swarm of bees approaching us. Then I saw it: hundreds and hundreds of scooters driving up to the intersection and coming to a stop at the red light right in front of us. I was mesmerized.

A few days later, I stood in a motorcycle shop in Peitou and handed over a stack of New Taiwanese dollars to buy my own scooter. She was purple, small—only 50cc—and secondhand, and she was perfect for me. She gave me wings. But not before I learned to face fear.

"Do you know how to ride a scooter?" the owner asked.

I shook my head. "No."

I'd never ridden a motorcycle or a scooter. Not in Taiwan, not in South Africa, not anywhere.

"You'll be fine," my housemate said. He flashed a big, confident smile. "Just follow us."

It was my first week in a new city, in a new country, on a new continent, in a new culture. I didn't know if I was coming or going. I was jet-lagged. I was reeling from all the new sounds, new customs, and a language so completely different from any language I'd ever studied. Everywhere I looked it was impossible to deny I was in a foreign-to-me country. I took a deep breath of the humid air.

We were at least forty minutes away from our apartment. It suddenly dawned on me that I had to drive that little purple scooter home. No lessons. No practice runs. Just get on and get going.

I felt terrified. My hands shook and my heart thumped as I took the key. I was waiting for more instruction, perhaps a gentle initiation into driving it in a quiet back alley, but before I could think, my friends began driving off. There were no mobile phones yet. I didn't have a map. I didn't speak the language, and I had no idea where we even were. I realized very quickly if I didn't get on and just get going, I would be completely lost. There was no time to think. Just turn the key and go, go, go!

I white-knuckled that ride all the way to the apartment, weaving through traffic, my hands shaking even as I held on to the handlebars. Fear sat thick and heavy, right on my chest.

But I did it. And I kept getting back on that little purple scooter. Every time I did, I became a little more confident. I learned how to navigate the traffic. Many days I rode with a city map right on my lap, but over time I learned my way around the city. I navigated the main arteries and found my way through back alleys. I was afraid many days, but I was learning I could move through it. I had to. In a completely foreign country, I slowly learned the way. Without knowing it at the time, getting on that scooter was my ticket to freedom. One day as I rode across the Chongyang Bridge into Shilin, a profound sense of freedom flooded my being. In that moment, I felt connected to the largeness of the universe and fully and completely alive. My heart was singing praises. I was beginning to find my way in this new world.

* * * * *

Leaving whiteness and entering an anti-racist world were, for me, like moving to Taiwan. I didn't know the lay of the land.

I didn't know how to get around. I didn't know the language. I was a newcomer.

This is exactly where recovery from our internalized racism happens. Squamish author and designer Ta7talíya Nahanee created a Decolonizing Process Map[2] by which she reminds us that it is only when we enter the work that we are actually decolonizing and dismantling. It might feel like a maze. It can feel disorienting. But the only way to do the work is to get on the scooter and join the traffic. We can't stand on the sidelines and think we are doing the work. We can't just talk about it. It is in actively learning, walking, and being with others that the old consciousness gets dismantled. We have to get on our purple scooters, get into the streets, and follow those who know how to get home. We have to leave the comfort of the old ways and set our heads and hearts toward liberation.

Several years ago, in a workshop hosted by Bautistas por la Paz, an organization whose mission is to be a witness to God's peace rooted in justice,[3] I learned about comfort, discomfort, and alarm zones.

In the comfort zone—our white cocoon of comfort—there's little learning. Life is boring, easy, and safe. The other extreme is the alarm zone. In this zone, learning and unlearning feels overwhelming, difficult, and terrifying. There is very little learning in the alarm zone. Ideally, we want to land in the discomfort zone. Here the journey feels scary, yes, but also challenging. This is where the learning happens, as we journey through. Fear will still show up, telling us to navigate the learning perfectly and not make any mistakes. Thankfully, there are wise ones who name "perfection" as the voice of the oppressor.

Cornel West says, "It takes courage to interrogate yourself. It takes courage to look in the mirror and see past your reflection to who you really are when you take off the mask, when you're not performing the same old routines and social roles. It takes courage to ask—how did I become so well-adjusted to injustice? It takes courage to cut against the grain and become nonconformist. It takes courage to wake up and stay awake instead of engaging in complacent slumber. It takes courage to shatter conformity and cowardice."[4]

It takes courage to get on our purple scooters and enter this new land. The moment my old apartheid lenses were shattered, I found myself in that wilderness that lies beyond whiteness. I had no framework. I didn't know which way was up, down, right, or wrong. My compass for being human had been shattered. I'd wanted to be a good person, even a good Christian, but what I had learned from whiteness about being good or successful was no longer compatible with being a decent human being.

Entering the wilderness meant leaving the dominant worldview. We exit the status quo. It feels uncomfortable and disorienting, because it's supposed to. The wilderness is meant to do its work in us. We come here to shake off Egypt and the pyramids of hierarchy we have learned. We come to the wilderness to rid ourselves of our pharaoh mentalities. We are meant to camp out here, live out here, make our lives out here so that the lies of that old white supremacy thinking can be snuffed out. We come to unlearn colonialist mindsets. Greed gets met by El Shaddai, the One who supplies all our needs, but not all our wants. Our hunger for power, place, and position is displaced by a hunger for service. In the wilderness is where we detox from whiteness.

The wilderness is also an invitation to newness, to relinquishment, to shedding the yokes, and to imagination. The wilderness that lies beyond whiteness calls us to love, relationship, and a new way of being human. May the discomfort of the now liberate us, and may the old ways of Egypt—the ways of the slave master, the tyrant, and the oppressor—drop right off. We are learning a new way of being.

Every day on this journey of recovering from our racism is a day to get on our purple scooters. May we make our way toward love and liberation.

Station of Discomfort

Leaving whiteness is not a one-time thing. In the beginning, especially, we may have to choose to leave whiteness and our white ways behind over and over again. We have to unlearn the ways of Egypt. Out beyond the rubble of our old constructs of understanding is where our long walk takes place. It will likely feel like a kind of wilderness, where every step is inside our discomfort zone. We might as well get comfortable with discomfort. Still, every time we choose to leave whiteness behind and walk through a gate of learning and unlearning, we add our intention, action, and resolve to create a different world with others.

▷ REFLECT

- What is your purple scooter story? How can that anchor you on this journey of recovering from racism?
- How does your body react to discomfort? How can you support your body on this journey of recovery so that it gains the ability to stay in discomfort?
- What are you most afraid of on this journey of recovering from racism?

The journey of the recovering racist is a journey of getting comfortable with our discomfort.

5

FACING UGLY TRUTH

White people, how does it feel to be a problem?

—Dr. Chanequa Walker-Barnes[1]

I imagine that one of the reasons people cling to their hates so stubbornly is because they sense, once hate is gone, that they will be forced to deal with pain.

—James Baldwin[2]

On April 27, 1997, I walked into a giant ballroom in Taipei to celebrate Freedom Day, the national day of South Africa. Elaborate chandeliers hung from the ceilings, and servers walked around with tall glasses of South African wines. The brand-new South African flag hung proudly in the room.

I'd grown up with words like *boycotts* and *sanctions*. During apartheid, the government was consistently called out by rock stars, celebrities, and international sports teams who refused to play in South Africa. As a teenager, I didn't know any other reality. I just accepted that we would likely not see U2 in concert in Cape Town. But then the apartheid government ended and our country crossed a threshold—transitioning to a democracy and becoming the darling of the world.

That night, as a young journalist reporting on the event for the *China Post*, I mingled with ambassadors, diplomatic representatives, Taiwanese government officials, the business elite of Taiwan, and other journalists. We were celebrating South Africa's emergence out of the dark story of apartheid. Nelson Mandela was our president. We now had eleven official languages. We sang "Nkosi Sikelel' iAfrica" as our anthem. We had a brand-new democracy.

We were now an "us," I believed. Deep lines used to separate us, but now we had started a journey together as the Rainbow Nation. We were a message to the world—a song of freedom, a song of possibility. That day, in that room, it felt like the world was celebrating with us. I stood proud of our national anthem, feeling giddy with how the world now loved us. There was a glorious freedom in the air, even in a fancy Hilton ballroom in Taipei.

But then something shifted in me. As I shook hands with guests that night, making introductions and doing my work, I suddenly became mindful of my accent. I was speaking English, but with my thick Afrikaans accent. Then, as I stretched out my hand one more time, it suddenly dawned on me: this international diplomat is hearing my Afrikaans accent. He knows that I am an Afrikaner woman. He's not a fool. He knows that Afrikaners implemented apartheid. I might be South African, but in the eyes of these global citizens, I am a white South African; and not just a white South African but an Afrikaner woman. I was not the darling of the world. In fact, I was despised. Warm shame washed over my entire body.

I had entered the room that night feeling so proud to be South African. But I left feeling ashamed that I was an Afrikaner. We were the villains. People in that ballroom were celebrating freedom *from* us. From me. From what I represented.

From what my people had done. History did not remember us kindly. I felt naked and deeply ashamed.

* * * * *

I didn't know what to do with the shame. I didn't know how to process it. White Afrikaners did not talk about it. People talked about food and wine and rugby, the weather and the next *braai*. As if nothing had happened. As if nothing had changed. And in some ways, little *had* changed for white South Africans after apartheid. We still shopped at the same stores. Went to the same schools. Lived in the same houses. Kept the same jobs. We also had a Black president and Black cabinet members, anyone could vote, and the world loved us. The Springbok rugby team could now play anywhere in the world, and we could even host the Rugby World Cup on South African soil.

I once saw myself as part of that story of glory—that peaceful transition to democracy. I wanted to be part of that story. But a different story had been written into the history books. More important, it had been written into the lives and the suffering of millions of people in South Africa. That night, on Freedom Day, I faced the shadow in my story. I could have kept it hidden, but I knew I was a truth-teller. And for me to be honest about my life, I knew I had to enter that shadow side and turn on the light. I had to stand and face the ugly truth.

Who was I now? How evil had my people been? What was mine to take on? How could I move through this? What was I to do with all this shame? I didn't know how to wash it off, scrub it off my skin and heal the past. I had no idea how to move forward. But that night, as a twenty-four-year-old white Afrikaner woman living in Taiwan, I began my search.

* * * * *

"South Africa is one of the most unequal countries in the world," said a 2018 World Bank report. "If you delve deeper into the dynamics of the South African society, you will realize how life is hard for the majority of blacks," writes Takudzwa Hillary Chiwanza.[3] Despite considerable progress in poverty reduction after the end of apartheid in 1994, the report found that the top 1 percent of South Africans own 70.9 percent of the country's wealth. The bottom 60 percent of the country control 7 percent of the country's wealth.[4] The World Bank has also found that intergenerational mobility is low, which means that "inequalities are passed down from generation to generation with little change over time."[5]

I was the intended beneficiary of this system. Standing in a ballroom in Taiwan, I was faced with the compounding consequence of colonialism, as well as forty-six years of apartheid, created, endorsed, enforced, and perpetuated by my people. I did not know how to process that. Years later, someone gave me a book telling the story of Yvonne Johnson, a Cree woman.[6] Yvonne's story gave words to some of my deepest longings— that people would not only awaken to themselves but would also awaken to all the peoples in the world. Her words gave me the courage to start sharing some of the shame—not for my own benefit but for the awakening to our belonging to each other. This was my heart.

● ● ● ● ●

"Are you sure you don't mean white guilt?" a friend asked many years later when I mentioned white shame.

I understood why she'd asked, and I took time to reflect on the question. I realized that racism was not something I only felt guilty about. Racism was not just in the history of my country; it was connected to my cultural identity and therefore to my personhood. I didn't just feel guilty about what my people had done. I felt deeply ashamed of who I was—and who I belonged to—in the world.

Guilt says, "I did something wrong."

Shame says, "I am something wrong."

When shame washed over me, being a white Afrikaner felt like *being* someone wrong. It was so different from the Afrikaner pride I was raised on.

"There is a profound difference between shame and guilt," says Brené Brown. "I believe that guilt is adaptive and helpful—it's holding something we've done or failed to do up against our values and feeling psychological discomfort. I define shame as the intensely painful feeling or experience of believing that we are flawed and therefore unworthy of love and belonging—something we've experienced, done, or failed to do makes us unworthy of connection."[7]

Racism felt unspeakable. It was not something white South Africans in my circles talked about or even named. It had to be hidden, but in the darkness, it only kept growing in power. "Shame derives its power from being unspeakable," Brown says.[8]

What my people had created and done and my participation in and benefit from it, both knowingly and unknowingly, made me feel like I, as an Afrikaner person, was unworthy of belonging in the story of South Africa. Even more honestly, I felt unworthy of love and belonging in the story of the world.

Shame, thankfully, is not where the story ends. Shame, for me, was a messenger. It showed me that how we had treated people and lived out a substantial portion of history was an offense to God. I knew I did not want to remain in that warm wash of shame. Nor did I believe I was meant to stay there.

"Shame is a feeling of regret, embarrassment, and disgrace, as the result of our guilt or shortcomings," says Mannette Morgan. "Unfortunately, over time, our shame can evolve into humiliation. People who accept humiliation as belief often become long-term victims as they find themselves ashamed and embarrassed of themselves and their past."

White people are not victims in the story of racism, but I have noticed how many white people have become stuck in that victim mentality. Whereas Brené Brown suggests we talk about our shame, Morgan suggests we face the shame and move it to guilt so that we can do something and not stay stuck in shame.[9] I suggest we do both: talk to other recovering racists about the shame tied to identity and also move the shame to guilt, so we can begin to make things right. As strange as it might sound, recovering from our racism is, in fact, an invitation to compassion, healing, and forgiveness.

Let's be clear: it is not a forgiveness required from those who have been harmed. Black, Indigenous, and People of Color do not owe white people forgiveness. What I am talking about here is taking on our own inner journeys of forgiveness. I had to forgive my ancestors. I had to forgive politicians and school principals, history teachers and pastors. I had to take an inventory of hurt and who I wanted to blame for all this. And then I had to find mercy for myself. When it comes to race-based shame, I found this idea very helpful.

So, what was my responsibility? How could I help make things right? I didn't know, but I knew I needed to find out.

●　●　●　●　●

A few months ago, a dear friend who was born and raised in Zambia sent me a beautiful video message for my birthday. "Our grandfathers would be proud of us," he said.

I cherished his words but also wondered if my ancestors would *actually* be proud of me. I wondered if they would be ashamed of this Afrikaner daughter who didn't set her Afrikaner-ness above her larger belonging to humanity. This Afrikaner daughter who wasn't proud of our people's history. This Afrikaner daughter whose kids don't speak Afrikaans. I longed for my ancestors to be proud. But I also remembered their racism. I ached for them to be anti-racist. I longed for a different story.

For several weeks I wrestled with the question of whether they'd be proud of me. Then one day while unloading the dishwasher, it dawned on me that my ancestors had all passed on. They had crossed the threshold into the place of love. I realized that being in the place of full knowing meant they no longer saw the world with racist eyes; they saw with eyes of love and justice. In the presence of the Holy One, they saw clearly.

They would want me to do this work, I thought. They would want these words to pour out from my heart and my mouth and my lungs. They are actually cheering me on.

This new understanding felt audacious. Could white ancestors who used to be racist now be part of my cloud of witnesses, like the book of Hebrews talks about, who cheer me on in anti-racist work? Were these my own thoughts? I wanted it to be true. It certainly felt true.

A few days later, I read how Swinomish elder Ray Williams spoke at the funeral of Susan Hutchison, a direct descendant of President Thomas Jefferson. Hutchison had helped start Coming to the Table, an initiative to bring together the children of formerly enslaved people with the children of those families who had enslaved people. As Williams spoke, he encouraged us to "conduct our lives so that the ancestors know we are paying attention." Then he added this: "They are in a place of pure knowing."[10]

Williams's words affirmed my thoughts from a few days earlier. I wanted to dance around the kitchen table. This meant my ouma—and anyone I loved who had passed on—would no longer see the world through racist lenses. I felt alive with the fresh revelation and finally felt connected to—not separated from—my ancestors.

On this earth, we know only in part, but our ancestors— our cloud of witnesses—see clearly. For them, all the veils have been lifted, including the veils of racism, white supremacy, hierarchy, and greed that still dim our vision. I imagine they are sitting together at the tables of grace and mercy, feasting on love together. They are cheering us on as we walk through this wilderness of liberation. We have a chance to live differently.

The shame around racism can make us defensive, drown us in denial, or shut us right down. If shame derives its power from being unspeakable, then to disarm it we need to lean right in to it. We name the shame of racism—this ugliness in our human story and the ugliest stuff within our souls, and even our bodies. We name it with courage, humbly. We don't have to run; we don't have to prove what good white people we are. We acknowledge the past. We face it. As we do the work, we can learn to write a different story.

Station of Facing Ugly Truth

"How does it feel to be the problem?"

Reflect on Walker-Barnes's question for white people.

What ugly truth do you still need to face? Don't try to solve it. Stay with it, wrestle with it in your own way until something breaks through. Keep your revelation in a safe place in your heart or journal or share it with your safe group of recovering racists.

Author Erwin Raphael McManus writes, "The question is not, 'Who are you?' That's simply the result of taking time to identify the material. The question is, 'Who will you decide to become?'"[11] We don't get to choose the skin we are born with, but we do get to choose what kind of person we will be inside it. Will I allow the complex questions of this time to pierce me and do their work in me? Facing the ugly truth of what whiteness has done—and our part in it—is an invitation to a different way. When we stand here, naked, honest, and even ashamed, we show up for the journey of transformation. We do it because at our very core love compels us to do whatever it takes to create a different world.

▷ REFLECT

- What is the ugly truth of your people?
- Do you feel ashamed about being white or what whiteness has done? How does it show up for you?
- Where do you feel that shame in your body? (If any of this is too overwhelming, please be sure to see a professional.)
- How can you move shame to guilt?
- Who is a safe person—a fellow recovering racist—you can share your ugly truth with? When you are ready, connect with that person to set up a time and safe container for sharing your ugly truth.
- Which ancestor is cheering you on the loudest?
- What is one beautiful truth about you?

The journey of the recovering racist is a journey of facing ugly truth.

6

THE LIBERATING JESUS

Dear ones,
Beware of the tiny gods frightened men
Create

—Hafiz[1]

When I left South Africa, I didn't want anything to do with a Jesus who endorsed colonialism, the slaughter of Zulu people, and the whole system of apartheid. I didn't leave the true Jesus in South Africa—just *white* Jesus.

In Taiwan I discovered that Jesus was alive and well, especially around a table of women at the Women's Power Breakfast. I showed up Wednesday after Wednesday to get to know this very different Jesus. The freedom I'd felt in the air on the day of the first democratic election in South Africa was also right there in downtown Taipei on a Wednesday at 7:00 a.m.

This was a liberating Jesus, a Jesus who loved all people, had joy, was brown-skinned, laughed, and turned over tables of injustice. It was a Jesus who flipped hierarchies of worth and said the last shall be first and the first shall be last. Over the months, as I began falling in love with this very different and yet authentic Jesus, I had a big question. It was something just between us. I figured the God of the universe, who was also deeply intimate, could handle the question of a young woman wrestling with her faith.

So I asked, "What's the big deal about the cross, God? Could you please help me understand?" I had been so disillusioned by my childhood church that I couldn't accept hollow definitions or explanations. I longed for a revelation.

Then one Saturday afternoon I walked into a fancy bookstore in Taipei with big glass windows and wooden floors. Classical Chinese music played softly over the speakers. I was not only browsing but also praying for God to meet me in that place. I noticed a book and pulled it off the shelf. It was a book about symbols with beautiful illustrations and short explanations about each symbol. There was a star. A triangle. A heart. Then I flipped another page: a cross.

My heart missed a few beats. Would the Jesus of the Bible meet me in the pages of a slim, green book on symbols? In a bookstore in Taipei? It wasn't even a *Christian* bookstore. Then I read the definition: the cross "universally symbolizes the process of relationship and integration."[2] A universal symbol of *relationship*.

Tears sprung to my eyes. I was the young woman who had felt the warm wash of shame not that long ago in a ballroom in Taipei. I carried that shame about being an Afrikaner and the legacy of apartheid in my body. My people had done the opposite of relationship: we had separated, restricted, and tried to extinguish relationship. The more I looked at that drawing of a cross, the more I saw the God of relationship. Not separateness. Not apartheid. But connectedness. Relationship. Community. Love.

God cares about apartheid, I thought. Jesus died for the sin of apartheid. Jesus died on a rugged cross to reconcile everything and everyone:

To reconcile our vertical relationship—with God.

To reconcile our horizontal relationships—each one of us
with each other.

Jesus suffered and died to bring us all together again. To make
wholeness. To bring close what we had ripped apart. Everything
converged in a person, both human and divine, crucified and
hanging on the very symbol of relationship.

God chose to speak to me, a daughter of apartheid, of separateness, of shredded relationships, about the cross in terms of
the wholeness of relationship. Redeemed relationships. Beautiful, whole, restored humanity. I was overcome by this God,
the great Rightmaker of our souls, our lands, our stories, our
relationships. The God of the universe chose a cross to become
a bridge not only between us and God but also between us and
each other.

This Jesus gave me the courage to keep going, to keep traveling down roads that pointed back to the injustice of racism
and forward to a more beautiful and beloved community of
humanity. I discovered my faith was always meant to be a part
of anti-racism work. More importantly, anti-racism was always
meant to be a part of my faith.

● ● ● ● ●

By 2042, for the first time in US history, white people will no
longer be the majority group. The Census Bureau announced
this projection in 2008, the same year President Barack Obama
was elected the first Black president of the United States.[3] It
triggered what many have called a *whitelash*,[4] a term coined by
CNN commentator Van Jones. *Cambridge Dictionary* defines
it as "a strong negative reaction to a change or recent events
by white people against the success and achievements of black
people."[5] Not only is it white people who are embodying this
whitelash; many claim to be followers of Jesus. But it is not

Jesus of Nazareth they follow; it's white Jesus. White Jesus is an idol, a false image, an imagination held up by whiteness.

Followers of white Jesus have been up in arms, even storming the Capitol in Washington, DC, on January 6, 2021, carrying Confederate flags and hanging nooses. How very tragic when Jesus, the Savior of the world we follow, had brown skin.

As much as I long for the reconciliation inherent in the cross, there is much work to do before we can get there. "The Black body sees the white body as privileged, controlling, and dangerous," writes trauma therapist Resmaa Menakem in *My Grandmother's Hands: Racialized Trauma and the Pathway to Mending Our Hearts and Bodies*.[6] White bodies in our world have not been safe for Black, Indigenous, and People of Color. White bodies have also carried their own histories, reflecting the energies and lies of white supremacy. Each one of us has work to do to make our own bodies safe so that over time, eventually, hopefully, white bodies will no longer represent danger to others.

I long for my white body to become a safe place for Black bodies, Indigenous bodies, and other bodies of Color. Making my white body safe asks me to work on healing trauma—ancient and new, personal and collective—lodged in my own body. It means I read, listen to, and learn from a wide range of voices, centering Black, Indigenous, and voices of Color. It means paying attention when I have a reaction or a response in my body to something that challenges whiteness or white heteronormativity. It means signing up for new courses on anti-racism or active bystander training. It means practicing what to say and speaking up against racist behavior. It means often feeling awkward and staying in the discomfort. It also means checking in with my heart. It means paying attention to shame rising in my body. For me, it also means contributing financially to the creative work of Black, Indigenous, and People of Color.

We come with our bodies, our senses, and our hearts to this work—not only with our minds. There are no checklists or to-do lists. We must find our way in the world in a new way. We do know this: whatever we heal now will not be passed down to the next generation. We are healing personal wounds as well as collective wounds. We are healing new wounds as well as ancient wounds. The white parts of the body of humanity need to rip out the lies, embedded within, so that we may be a part of the healing of humanity's wounds.

White Jesus has done so much harm across history. He is a false god who needs to be pulled down and destroyed. By grace, Jesus in a brown body, resurrected for all humanity, is good news for all bodies—including white bodies. Jesus speaks new life and resurrection to every one of our old skin stories.

Hallelujah.

Station of the Liberating Jesus

White Jesus has done so much harm. Be mindful of how white Jesus is used as an image of colonization, including how he was used at church-run residential schools for Indigenous children. Sit with that pain.

If you feel comfortable, imagine yourself sitting next to Jesus, not as a white-washed image with blue eyes and light-brown hair but as a person with brown skin. Imagine your body in proximity to his. His skin, your skin. Think about the spaces between you and Jesus. Stay there until you feel ready to leave.

The cross was meant as a symbol of shame. But through the cross, Jesus restores us to relationship. Reflect on the words in Psalm 34:5: "Those who look to YHWH are radiant, and their faces are never covered with shame" (IB). Are you still carrying any shame of racism? What can you do with it? (If you need to, go back to chapter 5.) Keep bringing any shame to liberating Jesus so that he may restore you to wholeness and even radiance.

▷ REFLECT

- Why do you think Jesus cares about racism?
- Where does the liberating Jesus want to meet you today?
- Reflect on the cross as a symbol of relationship, both horizontal and vertical. What does it mean to you?
- What does Jesus's brown-skinned body say to your skin? How is it good news for you today?
- What does an anti-racist faith mean to you?

Recovering racists follow the liberating Jesus.

7

THE HEART OF A LEARNER

I read the Bible and God [does] not approve of Ahab taking land from Naboth. So I don't think that God is pleased with the way the government has taken our land.

—Arthur Wellington Clah, hereditary chief of the Tsimshian Nation and Methodist missionary (1831–1916)[1]

In times of change learners inherit the earth; while the learned find themselves beautifully equipped to deal with a world that no longer exists.

—Eric Hoffer[2]

Conquer.

Appropriate.

Seize.

Colonize.

Commandeer.

Secure.

Take over.

Colonization is the "action or process of settling among and establishing control over the indigenous people of an area." It is also "the action of appropriating a place or domain for one's own use."[3]

Settlers, colonizers, and descendants of the main colonizing nations in the world—England, Portugal, Spain, the Netherlands, France, and Belgium—learned how to establish control. To take at any cost and appropriate places and domains for their own use. For six centuries, we, like fish swimming in water, have been comfortable with this language of power and making it central to a particular image of success. Taking, controlling, asserting force, dominating.

There has to be a new way for how we enter spaces, countries, and conversations.

* * * * *

On November 10, 1999, I landed at Vancouver International Airport with two suitcases and a ski bag full of clothes and belongings. As I walked through Canadian Immigration, I was crossing a threshold: entering a new country, on a new continent, with a soon-to-be husband.

I had taken big leaps before, moving away from my Afrikaans community to study at an English university. Moving from South Africa to Taiwan and living there for nearly five years. But this move was about to be my boldest—and hardest—yet.

I joked about Canada as the land of milk and maple syrup, a kind of promised land. I thought of Joshua, conqueror of Canaan, who entered with instructions to be strong and courageous. I still identified with the Israelites, of course. It would be a while before I began seeing whiteness, like Egypt, as a symbol that shaped pharaohs and slave drivers. It would be a while before I perceived how we—white people—conduct ourselves as pharaohs.

As I crossed the threshold into Canada, the Spirit was beginning to unfold and forge a new story in my soul. A few weeks after my very first Christmas in Canada, I drove home one gray, wet morning after dropping off my husband, Scott, at work. We'd been married nearly two months, and the whirlwind of it all was settling down. As I drove across the No. 2 Road Bridge in Richmond, I looked out toward the restaurant where Scott worked, and it dawned on me: I had married a Canadian man. His life was here. His work was here. His family was here. We would likely never live in South Africa together.

Then another reality dawned on me: not only had I moved to Canada, but I had left South Africa. With the excitement of falling in love, I hadn't thought about that. But that morning, the reality of what I had chosen—and what I had relinquished—crashed over me like a tidal wave. I had to pull over to the side of the road. It was the first huge pang of loss.

Living in Canada, I no longer existed in a web of relationships. No friendships. No family. No acquaintances. I didn't recognize faces anywhere. It took *years* before I began bumping into anybody I knew in a grocery store or mall. These had all been things I took for granted.

That first year, while Scott worked in the evenings, I watched *Friends* and *Ally McBeal*. During the days, I slept, prayed, and journaled. It took more than six months before I had coffee with someone who wanted to be friends with me. I was shaped by a deep loneliness, stripped of ego comforts.

There was so much I didn't know. I didn't know culture, politics, sports, or history. I didn't know the TV shows, actors, songs, or hockey. I often felt out of sorts and out of place. In Taiwan, I'd felt like a thriving tree. In Canada, a different image kept coming to me: a tree chopped down to its stump. Now I can see it more clearly for what it was—a cutting from an old vine. Instead of entering a promised land, I had entered a place of nothing.

Day after day, as I drove down new roads—roads I had never before traveled on—I was learning that what I was practicing on the outside was shaping both a courageous faith and a humility on the inside. It was humbling to start life over again. It was also exactly what was needed. As Ojibway author Richard Wagamese writes, "In the rich soil of humility all things grow."[4] I was being made new, learning and growing into new ways of being and new ways of doing. I had to set down almost everything I thought I knew and everything I thought I had to offer in order to become who I needed to be in this world.

Here's something we don't talk about very often: for white people, leaving whiteness comes with loss. Of course, in any conversation about racial justice, the loss that white people experience is not the center of the story. What racism has robbed Black, Indigenous, and People of Color of is absolutely central in the conversation. However, I address loss here because this book itself is a side conversation, in the basement, and loss is an honest part of this journey. Loss is a consequence my forefathers did not anticipate, and yet it is a part of the story for the generations that follow a history of oppressing others.

There are now nearly half a million white South Africans dispersed around the world. I don't know if it's theologically correct to draw conclusions from that number or not. But I do think about the warning in Leviticus: "If you defile the land, it will vomit you out as it vomited out the nations that were before you" (18:28).

I think about that when I talk to my mom on FaceTime and as I watch her grow older from thousands of miles away. I think about that when I long to drop by for tea or help my mom with a need. I miss family. I've missed my niece growing up. I miss my friends. I think about that when my children speak English. I have lost language, culture, and people.

That said, I do not see myself as a victim of my ancestors' decisions, and definitely not as a victim in the story of racism. This is simply an honest warning that injustice not only causes incredible pain and suffering for those who are oppressed by it but also carries consequences for the descendants of the oppressors.

For too long, Black, Indigenous, and People of Color have paid the price and carried all the cost of racial injustice. We, as white people, have a choice now in how we move forward. A more beautiful story is being called forth.

We can ask, "What does love require of us?"

• • • • •

Imagine we are entering anti-racism as if we are moving to a new country. We don't know the land, but there are people who have lived here for centuries. There are people who know how things work. There are people who have become established, who have built houses and planted gardens. There are people who already know how to be human together. We are simply a cutting from the vine, someone who has crossed the threshold and is willing to begin again.

When we first enter, we don't come with expertise. We come with intrinsic gifts, yes, but we don't know how to use these here yet, in this new place.

We come as beloved—a human being worthy of love and belonging. No need to earn that.

There are things we will need to let go of. Old ideas, perceptions, ideals, ways of interacting, ways of belonging, and even ways of knowing. These things will take time to unlearn.

We come to this journey mindful of our ego *and* moving to a whole self. We will keep doing the inner work.

Our neediness cannot be the center of the conversation. When we mess up, we muster the inner strength to return to ourselves. Instead of reacting, justifying, defending, lashing out, or dissolving into our neediness, we receive correction. We become grounded in our true sense of love and belonging.

We don't come to the story entitled. We come to the doorway hungry, willing, and audacious. We come to this journey sober about our contribution to and participation in the suffering of humanity *and* with compassion for our humanity. We come humbly, with a good heart. We are learners here. Let's sit together in the back. There is so much we don't know.

Station of Learning

The posture of white people in anti-racism work is humility. Reflect on these words by Potawatomi author Kaitlin Curtice:

> The heart space that an ally should inhabit:
> There is so much I don't know.
> I want to learn more.
> I am ready to listen before speaking.
> There is so much I don't know.[5]

When you are ready, find a place—a physical place, a line on a piece of paper, or an image in your mind—that can symbolize a threshold. Take off your shoes, either physically or metaphorically. When you are ready, mark this moment of being willing to enter as a learner and not a knower. Express your willingness. Then step across the threshold.

It is time.

▷ REFLECT

- How do you want to enter a new world of anti-racism?
- How full are your arms? What do you need to set down in order to be present to the inner work?
- Which part of you needs to be a fixer or an expert? Why? What can you say to that part of you?
- Who are the teachers you need to listen to?

We walk the journey of the recovering racist
with the heart of a learner.

8

MUTUALITY

I've been considering the phrase "all my relations" for
    some time now.
It's hugely important. It's our saving grace in the end.
It points to the truth that we are all related, that we are
    all connected,
that we all belong to each other.
The most important word is "all." Not just those who
    look like me, sing like me, dance like me, speak like
    me, pray like me or behave like me.
ALL my relations.

—Richard Wagamese[1]

On June 16, 1976, global news outlets ran an image of a
Black student, Mbuyisa Makhubo, running through the streets
of Soweto. He is carrying twelve-year-old Hector Pieterson in
his arms. Antoinette Sithole, Hector's sister, is running next to
Mbuyisa as they try to get Hector to a nearby clinic. But it is already too late. The South African police killed Hector Pieterson.

Antoinette remembers Hector as sweet and quiet. He liked
karate. The church in his community showed Bruce Lee films

on Saturday mornings for fundraising, and Hector regularly saved up his money so he could watch the movie each week.[2]

On June 16, 1976, Hector didn't go to school. On that Tuesday morning, he joined thousands of students in his community to protest a new law that required all students in South Africa to be taught in Afrikaans. Today there are eleven official languages in South Africa, but at the time, the government decided to force every child in school to speak Afrikaans and to make it the official language of instruction.

This was an injustice, especially from a government that had already stripped Black, Indigenous, and People of Color of land, forced Black men to carry passes, and set up the education system in such a way that a Black person in South Africa was denied post-secondary education. There was frustration, anger, and resentment, and students rallied and organized what was meant to be a peaceful protest.

Hector wasn't supposed to be at the protest—he was too young—but his sister thinks he must have tagged along with the older kids in the neighborhood. The students didn't have weapons. It was illegal at the time for any Black person to own a weapon in South Africa. All these students had were their bodies and their voices. They sang liberation songs, carried giant posters, and marched together.

Then the police showed up with tanks and machine guns.

The police fired into the crowd.

Hector was killed.

In the photo that was shared around the world, Mbuyisa is running away from the scene with Hector in his arms. There is blood running from Hector's mouth. Antoinette's hand is in the air as if to say, "Stop! Don't shoot."

They were students. In their uniforms. Running away from the police. Carrying a dead boy in their arms. Hector was only twelve years old.

Hector Pietersen is South Africa's Emmett Till.

Hector Pietersen is South Africa's Tamir Rice.
Pause.
Breathe.
Honor the story.

● ● ● ● ●

Hector's unjust death was a few months before my fourth birthday. Hector's death, along with the injustice of making instruction in Afrikaans mandatory in schools, sparked protests across the country. The protests reached my hometown of Paarl, and the fear surrounding them made its way to our all-white neighborhood. South Africa declared a state of emergency, and the men in our neighborhood decided to patrol the area.

That night I stood in our hallway on a red carpet in my bare feet and watched my dad put a gun in his pocket. It was a dark night—the middle of winter in South Africa—and I felt overwhelming fear. Why did my dad have a gun? Why were my parents talking in hushed voices? I didn't understand. The injustice in the land was ripping through the country, and the fear was taking hostages in its grip, including a sensitive three-year-old girl from Paarl.

I didn't know it at the time, but as I watched my dad go out into the night, my story connected with the story of Hector Pietersen. All the fear I felt in my little body became an invitation for darkness to find me. I could feel the racism that had caused Hector's death move up from the waterways and into the pipes. I felt it in the airways and in the air I breathed. I had caught a glimpse of the thick darkness shaking and possessing our country, harming and killing innocent twelve-year-old Black boys in Soweto. I sensed the history of unjust transactions; I sensed the greed and corruption that soaked into the land, underneath the carpet, and underneath the foundations. The land was crying out with the blood of innocent people and the powers of white supremacy. I sensed those powers and principalities all about, swirling and turning. I sensed the magnitude of the evil. I felt the darkness of the world. I was only three years old.

More than forty years later, I am still carrying Hector's story—and the injustice of his death—in my heart. Apartheid had created a world that was too violent for a twelve-year-old Black boy in Soweto. Apartheid had created a world of violence that didn't protect the ones it had meant to privilege.

We are connected to each other.

A part of my toddler self went into hiding that night, deep within myself. She stayed there for a very long time because she had learned the world was not a safe place. It was not a safe place for Hector Pietersen. But he doesn't get to live and tell the story.

* * * * *

"Racism is spiritual," writes South African theologian Sandiswa Kobe.[3]

When I moved to Canada in 1999, I was deeply committed to my faith. I experienced God as a liberating God, but the more I prayed and learned and walked in faith, the more stuck I began to feel. I could not make headway on any of my personal dreams—dreams I believed were from God. *This is not how liberation is meant to go*, I thought. *Am I not supposed to become more free?*

I hadn't understood yet that racism is spiritual. Still, more and more I sensed that my liberation was tied to the story of South Africa. It felt chained, deep within my soul, to a history that was heavier and thicker than I could carry or understand. I didn't know what to name that weight. I was living thousands of miles away from South Africa, and it was already a decade after the first democratic election, and yet every morning, it seemed, God and I were talking about apartheid.

I didn't yet have a theology that clearly connected my personal story to the pain and oppression of the people of South Africa. Just intuition. It felt like I was being guided. I didn't hear any other Afrikaners talk about this. I didn't hear white people, either in South Africa or in North America, talk about the long-term effects of racism in their souls. I felt alone.

The only place I had to go was to the green chair in my office where I met God, the lover of people and a lover of justice. Every morning I kept showing up—relentlessly—asking God for revelation and then following the crumbs.

One day a friend suggested I read *No Future without Forgiveness*, a book written by former archbishop Desmond Tutu. It was the exact right book at the exact right time. But I still had so little capacity for consuming the truth about racism in South Africa. When it came to racial justice, it was like I had been fed milk all my life, and it was now time to eat solid foods. I had to grow up in my spirit, get my consciousness strong.

I read only about a page at a time, sometimes only a few lines. Some lines shook loose windows of understanding. Other words rattled old doors of perception. Line by line, uncompromising truth hammered away at the old constructs apartheid had created inside me. I grew into new understanding. I felt like I was building muscle.

Then I read what Tutu said about the first democratic election in South Africa: "White people experienced that freedom was indeed indivisible. I had kept saying in the dark days of apartheid's oppression that white South Africans would never be truly free until we blacks were free as well."[4]

His words resonated through my entire body.

Indivisible.

You can't divide freedom. You can't separate it. I *was* connected to this story. Tutu illustrates our connection with a scene from the Sidney Poitier movie *The Defiant Ones*: "Two convicts, one white, the other black, escape from a chain gang manacled together. They fall into a ditch with slippery sides. One convict claws his way nearly to the top and out of the ditch but cannot make it because he is bound to his mate who has been left at the bottom of the ditch. The only way they can make it is together, clawing their way out, up and up and eventually over the side wall and out." The former archbishop adds, "So too I would say we South Africans will survive and prevail only together, black and white bound together by circumstance and history as we strive to claw our way out of the abyss of Apartheid racism, up and out, black and white together. Neither group on its own could make it. God had bound us together."[5]

Oh, how I'd felt those chains in the privacy of my journals and my prayers. Reading those words felt like watching a wave of truth come from a distance, rising and swelling and finally coming right up inside me, crashing, breaking, and rolling into the depths of my being. It felt like waters of baptism, truth inside me—healing truth, truth setting me free.

Martin Luther King Jr. also wrote about this connectedness in his "Letter from a Birmingham Jail": "Injustice anywhere is a threat to justice everywhere. We are caught in an inescapable network of mutuality, tied in a single garment of destiny. Whatever affects one directly, affects all indirectly."[6]

I kept learning these truths from Black activists and spiritual leaders, but I was surprised not to hear white people talking about this. I became more convinced that white people's liberation was connected to the pain and injustice we had caused. We were the white convict chained to the Black convict in the ditch. But white people, as far as I could see, were denying the chains we had placed on others. We kept running around with soul weights while covering and numbing the pain.

Even the Bible affirms our connectedness. Paul's words in 1 Corinthians 12:26 are an entire sermon on mutuality: "If one part suffers, every part suffers with it; if one part is honored, every part rejoices with it."

White people are connected to the genocide of Indigenous people in the Americas.

White people are connected to the pain and dehumanization of slavery.

White people are connected to the pain and degradation of Jim Crow and apartheid.

White people are connected to the deaths of Hector Pietersen, Steve Biko, and Chris Hani.

White people are connected to the deaths of Martin Luther King Jr., Malcolm X, and George Floyd.

White people are connected to the Trail of Tears.[7]

White people are connected to the pain and violence of residential schools in Canada and boarding schools in the United States.

White people are connected to the pain and violence of missing and murdered Indigenous women and girls.

What have white people done with all that pain?

"Morally speaking there is no limit to the concern one must feel for the suffering of human beings," writes Abraham Joshua Heschel.[8] "In a free society, some are guilty, but all are responsible."[9]

It is time for white people to loose the chains. We've been tied to the oppression and injustice we have inflicted on others, but we have not done the work to get out of the ditch. It's time for us to grow up, do the work of emancipation, and come into our own liberation—loose the chains of racism, white supremacy, and every element of whiteness. It's time to become fully human.

●　●　●　●　●

When I began confronting my complicity in the story of race, I was given a gift. Without the gift, I don't know if I would have had the fortitude to keep going. In order to face the depravity, I also needed to be reminded of the goodness and beauty of my humanity. The gift came from Desmond Tutu. Through his work and his words, he introduced me to the concept of *ubuntu*, meaning "a person is a person through other persons."[10]

"Ubuntu is very difficult to render into a Western language," he writes. "It speaks of the very essence of being human. Someone who has ubuntu is generous, hospitable, friendly, caring, and compassionate. It is someone who shares what she has. It is to say, 'My humanity is caught up, is inextricably bound up, in yours.' We belong in a bundle of life." He adds, "It is not, 'I think therefore I am.' It says rather: 'I am human because I belong. I participate, I share.'"[11]

Ubuntu speaks to the relationships between us. It is a gift to the dry and desert places in our white souls.

I am because you are.

We are human together.

We belong to each other.

Ubuntu is a way to understand our place in the world—how there is room for every one of us. Our freedom and dignity are connected to the freedom and dignity of another person.

"The bedrock of the philosophy is respect for yourself and for others," says Mungi Ngomane in *Everyday Ubuntu*. "So if you're able to see other people, even strangers, as fully human you will never be able to treat them as disposable or without worth."[12]

I serve and love a God of ubuntu who loves every person, who sees our good and our humanity and calls us to a more beautiful way. This God reminds us that we belong to each other.

When you thrive, I thrive.

When you rise, I rise.

When you get free, I get free.

When there is justice for the oppressed, the oppressor is also set free.

We get to choose how we live in this world. We can think only about ourselves and our small circle of family, our cultural group, and the way we grew up, or we can become more expansive, remembering that we belong to all of humanity. We belong to something so much bigger than ourselves; we belong to a humanity that is so much larger than one person only.

Ubuntu helped me understand why I couldn't get away from apartheid. Ubuntu helped me see how my freedom is connected to the freedom of others. Mutuality says I'm connected to the story of pain and oppression and can't be free without taking responsibility. Ubuntu reminds me of my humanity and that I, too, belong to the beautiful human family. Because we all belong to each other, I, too, as a white woman, get to belong.

If racism is a power and principality that drives a hierarchy of being human, cutting us off from one another, then ubuntu is the opposite spirit. It is an expression of love, generosity, and belonging. Ubuntu makes room at the table. Ubuntu says, "Everyone's humanity matters. We all have a place in this story." Nigerian author Sophie B. Oluwole reminds us, "In traditional African societies, ubuntu is the starting point for all social relationships."[13] Not success. Not winning at any cost. But belonging to each other.

Station of Mutuality

Ubuntu is a guiding principle for being human in this world. But please, fellow recovering racists, let us not colonize, co-opt, or appropriate this beautiful idea. I am merely pointing to this idea, and I will join you at the feet of those who teach us how to live it out. I do believe it is a key ingredient in understanding and learning how we can be human together on this earth. Ubuntu was a gift to me, reminding me of my belonging. I believe it could be a gift to our global community, if we can respect and honor its origins. May we learn to live by its wisdom, and may we do it justice.

Do a search on the internet for ubuntu. There are plenty of videos by Archbishop Emeritus Desmond Tutu in which he explains it, as well as many others. Write down what you learn or share it with a recovering racist friend.

▷ REFLECT

- Who is your Hector Pieterson?
- What does it mean to you when we say, "We belong to each other"?
- Do you notice an impulse to want to "own" this idea of ubuntu or any other idea that was not passed down through your cultural ancestry? Be mindful of that tendency and resist it. We are in recovery from these tendencies to want to "own" anything valuable or beautiful, including cultural wisdom.
- Who do you belong to? Who would you rather not belong to? Why?

The journey of the recovering racist is a journey of mutuality, knowing that we, as the human family, belong to each other.

PART 3
REPENT

Practice of Liberation: Walking through the Valley of the Recovering Racists

The desert is that place in Scripture where we go to figure out who is who and what is real. It is the place where souls are revealed.

—Kris Rocke and Joel Van Dyke[1]

The Karoo is a semi-desert in South Africa that is close to my heart. As a young girl, I often drove through the Karoo with my parents to visit family in the Northwestern Province. The flat road stretches before you for hundreds of miles, and you see nothing but dry bushes, red earth, and lonely windmills. It is a place of seeming nothingness. This very emptiness shaped the landscape of my imagination. On this road I exclaimed, as an exasperated little girl, "*Dis net bossies, bossies, bossies!*" ("It's just bushes, bushes, bushes!")

I learned to love the Karoo—not for its dryness but for the patience and endurance it solidified in my spirit. It reminds me to long for a different world even when the current reality seems stark and hopeless. It reminds me that a different world is possible even when it feels like dry bones are everywhere.

We may have come to this place—the valley of the recovering racists—and we can see only bushes, bushes, bushes. We hear the land crying out for justice. We hear the land crying out for the acknowledgment of the pain and shed blood of Black, Indigenous, and People of Color.

It is a dry and weary land. Recovering from our racism takes place in a spiritual context. It is not a lush landscape. Here, internalized biases come to die. It is where the old ways drop off like the shedding of old white supremacy skin. It is where we grow up into our humanity and where we build the capacity to stand for a new world. It is where we become the people we need to be.

This is the valley of the recovering racists—the landscape for becoming racially sober. Here, the Spirit asks, "What do you see?"

We see desolation.

We see dead dreams and broken lives.

We see communities destroyed.

We see knees on necks and bodies on the streets.

We see lives pierced and families separated.

We see injustice.

We see offense.

We see impossibility.

We see pride and ego.

We see hunger for power and control and greed.

We see isolation and poverty.

Like Ezekiel, we wonder, *Can these bones live, God? Can white bones become anti-racist? Is there any hope of change in the hardest of hearts?*

Then I am reminded of looking out the car windows as a young girl. The landscape looks bleak. It's a landscape that wants to tell you it will never end. That this is how it will always be. This is the beginning and the end. It is a landscape of death and lost dreams. Bare. Sandy. Desolate. Vast.

It is in this place of impossibility—a valley of dry bones left by centuries of oppression—that the Spirit reminds us of resurrection hope. It whispers, "Do you believe?"

Let's be clear: this resurrection hope can't be rushed. This life—this robust newness—will be forged only over long, slow years. There is much to dismantle. Much to unlearn. So much to heal.

But we show up. We walk. We stay the course. As we do, the Spirit breathes new life into us. Bones begin to rattle. Sinews stick together in new ways. Ligaments lift. Muscles grow. What was separated and stripped and left lifeless is filled again with new life.

This desert walk is our invitation to newness. Can you see it?

Come, Holy Spirit, come. We are dried-up bones. "Come, O breath, from the four winds! Breathe into these dead bodies so we may live again" (Ezek. 37:9 NLT).

This is where our souls will be revealed.

▷ **REFLECT**

- Do you have any stories about the desert?
- What do you imagine the desert will teach you?
- What is the invitation for you here now?

The journey of the recovering racist is a journey through the valley of dry bones, holding on to resurrection hope.

9

REPENTANCE

Being a racial ally means you are going to make mistakes
and stumble along the way.

—Anneliese A. Singh[1]

I need to tell you about a big mistake I made on this journey.

In September 2001, I attended a Global Celebration for Women
in Houston, a gathering of about fifteen thousand women from
around the world to shine a spotlight on the global issues that
affect women. Thousands committed to speak out against gender injustice worldwide. The day after the huge gathering, I was
with a group of global faith leaders to spend the day in planning
and prayer.

Over the lunch hour, we gathered in small circles to pray
and fast for the end of violence against women. I ended up in
a circle with, among others, a woman of Color who was a faith
leader from South Africa. I'd met Pastor Joanne (not her real
name) in my mother-in-law's living room in Robert's Creek,
Canada. We'd sat around meal tables together. I felt a sense of
home, just being in her presence.

Then I found myself in that small circle with her in Houston, praying for global issues. We were praying for hard things, like human trafficking, the worldwide abuse of women, inequality, the abuse of power. When we started praying about systems of power and the abuse of power, the air around me became thick and heavy. I felt like I couldn't move forward in prayer. With every prayer, I became more aware of our shared history as South Africans and the divide that apartheid had created between us. I became hyperaware of my Afrikaner identity. I couldn't pray about power imbalance in the world without addressing the power structures that had created the landscape of division in South Africa. I felt like I couldn't pray for the oppression of women in our world until I had addressed how my people had oppressed.

I sank to the floor.

"I can't pray against the abuse of power without recognizing how my people abused power in South Africa," I said to her. "Please, forgive me. Please, forgive us."

She bent toward me and received my words.

"Unsolicited confessions [from white people to Black people] inspired by a sense of guilt are often poured over Black bodies in search of their own relief," says Austin Channing Brown in *I'm Still Here: Black Dignity in a World Made for Whiteness.* Brown experienced this "self-indulgent desire for relief" after an MLK Day celebration at church one day.[2] People lined up to speak to her. "On and on the confessions went, but none was healing to my soul," she says.[3] "Black women were bearing the brunt of these stories as white attenders sought relief from guilt over the ways they had participated in racism. . . . I was expected to offer absolution. But I am not a priest for the white soul. . . . White people really want this to be what reconciliation means: a Black person forgiving them for one racist sin. But just as I cannot make myself responsible for the transformation of white people, neither can I offer relief for their souls."[4]

That is exactly what I had done with Pastor Joanne.

Confession is an intimate act between two specific people for a specific harmful act. If I do something specific to harm someone, my faith compels me to make amends. When it comes to racism, we are dealing with systemic wrongdoing against a collective people. What we as white people often do—however well intended and perhaps even inside of relationship—is find a Black person, an Indigenous person, or another Person of Color and pour out our individual confessions for our collective sins to that individual. By doing that, we continue the harm. Repenting of a specific sin against a specific person is part of repairing the past. But we cannot perpetuate the harm by making Black, Indigenous, and People of Color our priests, whether for our personal sins or for the collective sins of racism.

● ● ● ● ●

There is a place for repentance. I believe in bringing our bodies to places of historic oppression and repenting to God for the sins of our ancestors right where they happened. Not as a public spectacle but simply as something between us and God and the land.

In 2004 Scott and I visited South Africa. Our first daughter, Gabi, was nine months old, and we were excited to see family, drink Appletiser, and bask in some South African sun. I also knew I needed to go to Robben Island. Robben Island is a World Heritage Site off the coast of Cape Town. It is home to the jail where Nelson Mandela spent most of his twenty-seven years in prison before he became South Africa's first democratic president.

On that September morning, it was early spring in South Africa, and we knew the journey could be precarious. Cape Town is known for its southeasters—winds so strong that people have to cling to telephone poles to stay standing. As we boarded the boat, my heart beat wildly. My skin felt alert.

I sensed that this was a sacred journey—not just a tourist visit but a pilgrimage.

Robben Island holds the pain and the stories of more than three thousand political prisoners who fought for freedom from apartheid in South Africa. It is a place of profound injustice. The apartheid government justified its actions by labeling most prisoners held there as terrorists.

Malcolm X once said, "When a man whom they have been taught is below them has the nerve or firmness to question some of their philosophies or conclusions, usually they put that label [extremist] on us, a label that is only designed to project an image which the public will find distasteful."[5]

When we got off the boat, I immediately felt the weightiness of the soil, like a thousand anchors were pulling me down, down, down into the pain the land had held and witnessed over centuries. There was lead in my bones. The other people on the tour walked past, onward toward the prison and toward our tour guide, but I felt glued to the land. I could not walk on. I simply could not take another step on the land without repenting. I sunk to my knees on the rocks and the sand right then and there.

What have we done, O God? What have we done?

The words poured from me as I felt the weight of pain and injustice inflicted by my people. I felt the weight of apartheid—forty-six very long years of it—pulling at me from the ground. I knew I could never feel the full weight of it. And even a glimpse of it seemed too much to bear. Deep sorrow ripped through my body, and words of repentance for what my people had done poured out—first in English and then in Afrikaans.

Forgive us, O God. Forgive us.

Vergewe ons, Here. Vergewe ons.

I prayed as an Afrikaner woman for the sins of my people, begging God for forgiveness. I prayed for my own complicity in the injustice and how I had benefited from the pain inflicted on others. I stayed on the ground, knees bent before the God of the universe for a long time.

Finally, Scott nudged me. "They're going to start the tour. Let's go inside now." He held out a hand and helped pull me up. It was only the beginning of stepping further and further out onto a path of repentance.

● ● ● ● ●

The Equal Justice Initiative (EJI) has created a powerful site of repentance and lament for people to remember the violent history of racial terror lynching in the United States. At the National Memorial for Peace and Justice in Montgomery, Alabama, there are more than eight hundred Corten steel monuments—one for each county in the United States where a racial terror lynching took place. On each of the columns, the names of the victims from that county are engraved. According to EJI, more than forty-four hundred Black men, women, and children were "hanged, burned alive, shot, drowned and beaten to death by white mobs between 1877 and 1950."[6]

The memorial also has a living element. The Community Remembrance Project (CRP) invites visitors to get involved in truth telling about racial injustice and face their own local histories. Communities in which a lynching took place can apply to create a coalition, committing to the CRP values of narrative truth-telling, a trauma-informed approach, collaboration, and listening with respect. "Pay attention to what is and is not being said," they remind us. Another value is that of "just kindness"—a commitment to "consistently act and speak from a place of goodwill towards others."[7] Communities are invited to organize a soil collection ceremony, hold an essay contest for local high school students, and do active community remembrance work. In Bessemer, Alabama, for example, CRP members partnered with EJI to host a soil collection in honor of Hardy Posey and John Chandler, two of the four documented victims of lynching in that county.[8] EJI will collaborate with that community to place a monument—a replica of the column at the National Memorial—in the community itself. It is important to take our white bodies to places where whiteness and racism have caused such pain and terror. It matters to stand on the ground—not as a performative ritual but as a quiet act of repentance and healing. It matters to be a witness.

Perhaps I saw how a place could speak of the past when my dad took us to Dachau. Or perhaps I had already heard how the rocks were crying out for justice in South Africa when I was three years old and Hector Pieterson had died. I have been to enough places of pain in our world now to know that land can tell stories our minds don't always comprehend. We need to bring our bodies.

Resmaa Menakem speaks to white bodies when he says, "Your niceness is inadequate to deal with the level of brutality that has occurred."[9] There is no place for niceness when we walk through the gas chambers at Dachau or the prison cells on Robben Island. There is no place for niceness when we walk through the National Memorial for Peace and Justice, reading the names of the people who were lynched. In these places, it's clear that niceness is not adequate. It's an affront.

Instead, we need a repentance revolution. Not public. Not a show. But in the privacy of our kitchens, our bedrooms, our bathrooms. In the quiet prayers of repentance at sites of horror in human history. A repentance revolution can take place in the consistent, intentional, thoughtful unlearning of old racist ways and the consistent, intentional, thoughtful decisions to move toward justice and a new way of being human together.

●　●　●　●　●

"Repentance brings the hope of real healing," writes Latasha Morrison, founder of Be the Bridge, a nonprofit organization that equips thousands of ambassadors of racial reconciliation across five countries.[10]

Repentance, from the Greek word *metanoia*, means "to turn around, turn away from, change one's ways, change one's mind, and walk in a new direction."[11] Repentance requires more than words. We can't just talk about repentance. We have to do repentance by repenting. Repentance is taking our "sorry energy" and turning it into action. Repentance is doing justice. It is coming face-to-face with the systemic injustices of racism and owning our place in that story.

Repentance is a journey out of ego into heart. In 2 Chronicles 7:14 we hear a clear call to repentance: "If my people, who are called by my name, will humble themselves and pray and seek my face and turn from their wicked ways, then I will hear from heaven, and I will forgive their sin and will heal their land." Repentance is releasing the tight grip we may hold on our defenses and our sense of rightness. Repentance is dealing with hard-heartedness. A repentance revolution takes place on the front lines of our hearts.

Repentance is holding up a flashlight to the places where white supremacy ideologies have lodged and calcified in our bodies. Repentance allows the God of the universe to touch those hardened places with a tender hand. Whereas the Spirit of love binds up the wounds of the brokenhearted, love unbinds the hardened bits of an oppressor's heart. Like pouring warm water onto calcified grime, love washes away the stony pieces, the ugly rocks when we come in repentance.

Repentance is not the recipe for "success" so many of us have worshiped. But this is God's economy, and we are at the gates of love and justice, longing for entry into the kin-dom of God. For those of us who have had high seats at high tables and have sat at the center of the story for so long, coming on our knees is the requirement for entry. Here, repentance and humility kiss. We become human. Perhaps we are reborn. Isaiah 30:15 reminds us, "In repentance and rest is your salvation."

Jesus modeled the way of self-emptying and called us to repentance (Matt. 4:17). For some of us that means turning from our old white ways. The beautiful kin-dom way reminds us that as we empty ourselves, we also become ourselves, and we are connected to the humanity of every other person on this earth.

God meets us on our knees.

●　●　●　●　●

When we took the last boat back to Cape Town harbor that Monday afternoon in 2004, the seas were stormy, wind and waves shaking us. As I sat in the belly of the boat, I felt so sick. I was pregnant with our second child, but I was also sick with the history of racism and whiteness. I became sick on the boat, and after we walked off, I got very sick in a garbage can, right there on the pier.

My friend Fiona, a spiritual director and writer in the United Kingdom, says that when we make a pilgrimage, we look for the places of our resurrection. This requires emptying ourselves of old, oppressive ways of being and acting. Recovering from our racism requires dying to every last racist idea within.

Like the southeaster wind, may the winds of the Spirit blow us on pilgrimages to places of pain and injustice. May the Spirit make waves that shake our boats and cause us to empty ourselves of every last poisonous idea, every lie that was made to sound like truth, and every strand that upholds the systems and structures of white supremacy.

Kaitlin Curtice writes, "Who gains life when we deconstruct these systems of whiteness, white supremacy, and toxic patriarchy? Everyone. Who loses out when we refuse to take a deep look at our own toxic systems? Everyone."[12] Repentance creates new beginnings and calls us to change direction. It opens new doors and is felt down through the generations.

In 2017, on the last day of a trip to South Africa before returning to Canada, my kids and I were staying at a dear friend's home in Cape Town. That morning she had invited another friend to come over for breakfast. She was a Facebook friend—a renowned theologian, firecracker, and changemaker. Our kids were playing together while we sat at the table, eating scrambled eggs, croissants, and plates full of steaming bacon. I can still feel the warmth of laughter and the ease of friendship as we sat together that morning, sharing our lives and our families. Then, when she mentioned her mother, I was reminded again that she was Pastor Joanne's daughter. A new story was rippling through the generations. I quietly marked the moment in my heart and said, "Thank you, God." In spite of my past, my awkwardness, and my mistakes, I had been invited into a new story.

Station of Repentance

Do not harden your hearts, the psalmist reminds us (Ps. 95:8–9). Recovering from our internalized racism starts with a repentant heart. It is a heart that is soft toward God and soft toward people.

Layla F. Saad, author of *Me and White Supremacy*, says, "The system of white supremacy was not created by anyone who is alive today. But it is maintained and upheld by everyone who holds white privilege—whether or not you want it or agree with it."[13] We have a choice to continue upholding that oppressive system or turn away from it now, emptying ourselves of all of it, and learn a new way. The terror, danger, oppression, and trauma can begin stopping with each one of us.

▷ REFLECT

- How is your heart?
- What does repentance require of you on this journey of anti-racism?

- What do you need to empty yourself of?
- How can you turn your "sorry energy" into action without causing harm?

The journey of the recovering racist is a journey of repentance—turning away from our white ways and walking in a new direction.

10

SEEKING JUSTICE

If you have come here to help me you are wasting your time, but if you have come because your liberation is bound up with mine, then let us work together.

—Lilla Watson[1]

A few weeks before my thirty-seventh birthday and ten years after I'd moved to Canada, I read an email from a friend with updates about their trip through Kenya, Rwanda, and Burundi. They shared about a visit to a hairdressing school in one of the most economically poor neighborhoods in Nairobi. The hairdressing school was run by a local church, teaching women how to become aestheticians and hair stylists and to run their own small businesses. The school was doing well, and more women had applied than they could accommodate. In their email, my friend shared how the school had trouble paying the electricity bill.

How much would the electricity be? I wondered. I was a stay-at-home mom with three young kids. I worked as a host in a restaurant once a week. My life was full of activity, but something about that simple statement in that email wouldn't let go of me. I knew if I emailed back and asked about it, I would feel a sense of responsibility. Thanks to Archbishop Tutu, I also understood that I was connected to those women. So I took a breath, emailed my friend, and asked.

When I heard the number, I knew it was more than what I could cover myself. But I had a blog, and I'd seen friends do small acts of what they called "backyard philanthropy." It was about seeking justice and making the world a little bit more right. It was sharing what we had.

So, on my birthday that year, I sat on the red couch in our living room and asked readers to join me in supporting the hair-dressing school. Slowly but surely, donations began to roll in. Family members made donations instead of giving me gifts, and by the end of the day, one friend—a hair stylist in Canada—had committed to a monthly donation. Together we had covered the electricity bill for that hairdressing school for an entire year. Even though all I'd done that day was write a post and sit on the couch, I knew I'd become a part of something powerful.

Coming alongside those women in that community was about seeking a little more justice in the world. What I didn't expect, however, was how much more connected I felt in the world. I was astounded and humbled by how friends and family had rallied around me. My act on behalf of the women in Nairobi had met me in my own deepest wounds—that deep separateness inside me. As I took action that day, my belief in ubuntu and in our connectedness to each other grew.

I thought that was the end of the story.

At the time, while my justice consciousness was being shaped in Canada, the only relationships I had in South Africa were with white people. It was unacceptable to me that apartheid was still alive and well in my friendships and relationships in South Africa. I was hungry for conversations about reconcili-ation and healing across our racial divides in South Africa. I was so hungry that when I learned of a faith gathering outside Johannesburg in 2009, I sat in front of my computer following every tweet from attendees I could find. I learned that at the conference Adriaan Vlok, a former security minister, had washed the feet of a former soldier. During the apartheid years, the white soldier had been conscripted and still carried deep resentment toward Vlok.

When I learned that same conference—Amahoro Africa—was happening in Kenya in May 2010, I longed to go. I'd never set foot in any other African country. During apartheid, all flights on South African Airways were banned from flying across the continent.[2] After apartheid ended, I had felt too ashamed to visit. I didn't think, as a white Afrikaner woman, I had the right to enter. In my spirit, it felt like the gates into Africa had been shut. But the desire in my heart grew and grew.

Scott and I had planned for me to fly to South Africa that year to attend my twentieth high school reunion. Then, one night, while praying and pouring my heart out to God, I imagined my high school reunion: I pictured the room and which classmates would be there. I knew the entire room would be white, and I just didn't want to be in an all-white world any longer. I ran up the stairs as fast as I could and blurted out to Scott, "What if, instead of buying a ticket to South Africa in August, I go to the conference in Kenya?" Practically, it didn't make any difference, and he knew how important this journey would be for me. We agreed, and I bought a ticket to Kenya.

I will never forget landing at the airport in Nairobi—from where I would fly to Mombasa—very early on May 4, 2010. Walking off the plane, I read the sign for Kenya Airways: "The Pride of Africa." All around me I saw Black pride. I didn't feel worthy, and yet I also felt fully welcomed. I wanted to shout "Hallelujah!" I stood on the tarmac that morning and looked out across the landscape, watching the sun rise on a new day. Gates that had been shut tight for thirty-seven years were creaking open. I was welcomed to a new beginning on the continent of my birth.

It was a new day, indeed. I took a deep, grateful breath. This, too, was holy ground.

• • • • •

When I landed in Mombasa, a thick humidity hung in the air. Adrenaline was pumping through my veins. I felt like I had stepped inside a giant paradigm shift and my consciousness was being recalibrated. I found a seat in the back of the conference room and soaked up the presentations, ideas, and stories from theologians and practitioners who were mostly from East Africa but also a few South Africans. My body felt like it was both at home and being immersed in a new place.

Kelley Nikondeha, one of the founders of Amahoro Africa, and I had never met in person until that Tuesday morning. At the end of the session, we found a place in the back of the conference room and talked for hours. It was the beginning of a transformative heart friendship I treasure to this day. Days before I flew to Kenya, a small team had launched *SheLoves Magazine*, a website featuring stories of a global sisterhood rooted in justice. It was the dream I'd carried in my heart for more than ten years. It was also the dream that had been mired in molasses, the dream that couldn't move forward until I first began reckoning with my apartheid past. Now suddenly, it felt like my dreams and hopes were also coming true.

When Amahoro ended, I flew back to Nairobi and spent a few days in the city. I'd been invited to see the hairdressing school and meet the students. Sitting in that public bus and navigating Nairobi traffic, again I was overwhelmed with gratitude. Words—an email and a blogpost—had become flesh. My heart was walking around outside my body.

At the hairdressing school, we drank Fanta, and the women told their stories. We celebrated sisterhood and belonging. We were connected to each other. Their liberation was also my liberation.

The words of Lilla Watson, Aboriginal elder, activist, and educator from Queensland, Australia, rang in my heart.

Oh, how my liberation was bound to theirs.

●　●　●　●　●

After my trip to Kenya, Kelley and I began talking nearly every day, often more than once. We often talked about Communities of Hope, a nonprofit organization in Burundi run by Kelley's husband, Claude. She was always telling me about what Claude was up to and especially about the development project they had started in Matara outside Bujumbura with thirty Batwa families.[3] The Batwa people in Burundi are Indigenous and make up only about 2 percent of the population. They are often discriminated against and have also suffered from extreme poverty.[4] When the Batwa families in Matara began flourishing, Communities of Hope started another, much larger community development project—this time in the province of Bubanza—with over a thousand families. One day, toward the end of 2011, during one of our little chats, Kelley shared that many of the women in Bubanza did not have identity cards.

When she said "identity cards," something in my spirit perked up. I felt immediately connected to the story. As an immigrant, I remembered what it had felt like to apply for my immigrant status in Canada. Then I'd waited eight years before I applied for citizenship. I understood, in my own limited and privileged way, how much identity documents mattered.

I took a deep breath and then asked, "How many women need an ID card? How much does one cost?"

Our phones buzzed back and forth between Vancouver and Burundi. For $12, each woman in that community could get an ID card. For many women in North America, $12 didn't seem like a lot, but those $12 would allow our sisters in Burundi to vote, open their own bank accounts, and even access free medical care for themselves and for their children. A few weeks later we launched the first major campaign through the SheLoves community to raise money for ID cards for our sisters in Bubanza. We raised more than $7,000, and over six hundred people received their cards.[5] That meant every woman in Bubanza had an ID card. Soon, because these Batwa women were now able to vote, politicians also began paying attention to them as constituents. We were astounded at the power of one ID card.

A few months later, my friend Tina Francis-Mutungu and I flew to Burundi for another Amahoro Africa gathering. When we landed in Bujumbura, I had no idea what else Kelley and Claude had in store for us. All I knew was we were to go to Bubanza to be with the women and celebrate their identity documents.

When we arrived in Bubanza, we were ushered into an area where many people—mostly women—were gathering and singing. Kelley showed me to a seat. It was a plastic chair under an asbestos roof on a dirt floor, but it might as well have been a seat in the world's most beautiful palace. As she pointed to the chair near the front of the gathering, my whole body reacted. Shame rose up, and it was visceral. Voices inside said, "You are not worthy of a seat of honor in this holy place. You are a daughter of apartheid."

But the women around me, who knew my story and loved me, held that seat for me. Then Claude and the community leaders invited us to help with handing out the last two hundred ID cards.[6] We danced and celebrated and laughed—a beautiful global sisterhood united in mutual liberation.

I received my own identity card that day. Not a blue one, like the cards the women of Bubanza received, but one written on my heart that said "Daughter of justice." A new story was being written—both for the women in Bubanza and in my heart.

These stories of the hairdressing school in Nairobi and the ID cards in Bubanza were deep markers on my journey of becoming. I did not see myself as separate from these women's stories. My humanity was connected to their humanity. I saw—and felt—the tides of ubuntu. We were connected to each other's liberation. And isn't this what Micah 6:8 compels us to do? Seek justice, love mercy, walk humbly.

* * * * *

Nicole Joshua, a teacher at Cornerstone Institute in South Africa, helped crack open Micah 6:8 even more. She offered me a lens that has helped me immensely in understanding how to respond in an unjust world. Based on the work of Old Testament scholar Walter Brueggemann, Nicole has taught me that the text authorizes two distinct communities: Communities of Permission and Communities of Requirement.[7]

"Communities of Permission are communities who are oppressed, marginalised, and silenced," says Nicole. "When these communities approach the text, they find a God who is for them and they find themselves authorised to lament their injustice and cry against their oppression." Communities of Requirement, however, are "communities of the privileged," explains Nicole, "whether they are privileged physically, socially, politically, or economically. When these communities approach the text, they find themselves authorised to 'act justly, love mercy, and walk humbly with their God.'"[8]

This distinction has helped me so much. In situations that require a response, I can ask, "Am I part of the privileged community here?" If so, the requirement is clear: seek justice, love mercy, walk humbly. This is where I mostly find myself.

As a woman, in a world with a long history of oppressing women, there are times when I land in the Communities of Permission. As a woman, if I have been oppressed, marginalized, or silenced in a situation, the text authorizes me to lament and cry out. It is fully okay to be angry, cry out against injustice, and shout to the heavens.

However, when white people talk about race and racism, we always find ourselves in Communities of Requirement. The only thing Scripture authorizes us to do, then, is to seek justice, love mercy, and walk humbly with our God. Communities of Requirement are not authorized to question the lament, anger, or frustration of the people who belong to the Communities of Permission. Communities of Requirement are not authorized to lament about the injustice. Communities of Requirement are not authorized to cry out about the oppression. The only thing Communities of Requirement are authorized by the text to do in these situations is to seek justice, love mercy, and walk humbly with our God.

Let's remember this the next time we want to silence someone's anger. Let's remember this the next time we want to question the validity of someone's rant against racial injustice. Let's remember this the next time we hear someone's lament.

It is not our job to question those who belong to the Communities of Permission. They have God's permission. As white people, we have to learn to listen to pain. As white people, we have to learn to hold space for lament. As white people, we have to learn to be quiet.

Author James Baldwin, when asked by a radio host about being Black in America, once said, "To be a Negro in this country and to be relatively conscious is to be in a state of rage almost, almost all of the time—and in one's work. And part of the rage is this: It isn't only what is happening to you. But it's what's happening all around you and all of the time in the face of the most extraordinary and criminal indifference, indifference of most white people in this country, and their ignorance."[9]

● ● ● ● ●

Several years ago I watched an excerpt from *The Color of Fear*, a film by Lee Mun Wah about the state of race relations in America as seen through the eyes of eight North American men. While responding to "what it means to be American," one participant, a Black man, became very angry.[10] He was sick and tired of needing to adjust to the requirements of whiteness as a so-called standard.

He lamented, crying out against the injustice of racism. The white men in the group held space for his anger. They didn't question it; they didn't react; they simply listened.

As white people, it's crucial for us to learn to listen to anger. We need to be able to listen to the raw, unfiltered truth. No fixing. Just listening with compassion. Vietnamese monk Thich Nhat Hanh calls this "deep listening." "Deep listening is the kind of listening that can help relieve the suffering of the other person," he says.[11] We need to learn this kind of compassionate listening so that we can sit with the pain of humanity. So we can sit with the pain of injustice. It is a kind of listening that can help heal the wounds that racism has caused. Consider these words of Chrystos, a Menominee poet and activist:

> My knee is wounded so badly that I limp constantly
> Anger is my crutch I hold myself upright with it[12]

To be white in the story of racism is to listen to anger and to hold space for anger. To be white in the story of racism is to belong to the Communities of Requirement. What is required is simple: seek justice, love mercy, and walk humbly. It is simple but not easy.

Station of Justice

Sometimes the injustices of the world and humanity's pain can feel overwhelming. It would be easier to numb or hide. At times like that, I am reminded of these words:

> Do not be daunted by the enormity of the world's grief.
> Do justly, now. Love mercy, now. Walk humbly, now.
> You are not obligated to complete the work, but neither
> are you free to abandon it.[13]

Seeking justice is not an option when we are on the path of recovering from our internalized racism. Seeking justice is part of
our work of love. But it's important to examine our motivation:
Why am I seeking justice? If it's rooted in ego, step back. If it's
to be a hero, step back. The world doesn't need white saviors.
White saviorism "is a systemic and often deliberate practice that
centers whiteness as the heroes of the narrative," writes Nicole
Cardoza, founder of *Anti-Racism Daily*. She adds, "Whenever
you are advocating for a necessary cause, make sure you're
sharing work and resources from the communities impacted.
If any type of advocacy work centers the 'you' above the 'we,'
it's more harmful than helpful."[14]

We show up for justice and we seek justice, because we remember that our liberation, as humanity, is bound together.
Who is your liberation bound to? Where does your story intersect with injustice? That's where we begin, humbly.

▷ REFLECT

- What does it mean to you to seek justice, love mercy,
  and walk humbly?
- Where do you fit in the Communities of Requirement?
  What does that mean to you?
- Is there anywhere where you fit into the Communities
  of Permission? What does that mean to you?
- Can you remember a time when you listened to anger to
  help heal the wounds racism has inflicted?
- How does "white saviorism" show up for you?

The journey of the recovering racist is a journey of seeking justice.

PART 4
RECALIBRATE

Practice of Liberation: Remembering Joy

Joy is an act of resistance.

—Toi Derricotte[1]

Laughter is stronger than darkness.

—Steven Charleston[2]

This is a little reminder to remember joy. As we do the hard and holy work of anti-racism and recovering from our internalized racism, we also take time to remember our humanity.

What brings you joy?

Take time to dance in the kitchen or dig in the garden. Watch a sunrise or a sunset. Gather with friends and laugh. Make a toast to the beautiful and good things in life. Pet your dog or your cat or cuddle with a soft blanket.

When I read anti-racism books or take a course on anti-racism, I also have a book on hand that reminds me to practice self-compassion and intentionally spend time being gentle and kind to myself. I watch comedies, go for long walks in the forest, or bake bread. This way I can stay in the work for the long haul.

Before racism slithered into our human story, we were beloved. We still are. We just *also* have deep inner work to do.

So don't forget to do the things that remind you of love and joy. I can easily sink into a place where I beat myself up. That is not liberation. We are racially sober *and* we practice deep joy and delight at the same time.

▷ **REFLECT**

- What brings you joy?
- What helps you remember your belovedness?
- When was the last time you laughed? How can you bring more laughter into your life?

The journey of the recovering racist is a journey of remembering joy.

11
THE WAY
OF RELATIONSHIP

We cannot say that in the process of revolution someone liberates someone else, nor yet that someone liberates himself, but rather that human beings in communion liberate each other.

—Paulo Freire[1]

Let us find a way to belong to this time and place together. Our future and the well-being of all our children rests with the kind of relationships we build today.

—Chief Dr. Robert Joseph[2]

Moenie die pap te dik aanmaak nie. I grew up with this Afrikaans expression that means "Don't make the porridge too thick." It's an admonishment about relationships. Don't get too close. Don't spend too much time together. Keep people at a distance. Growing up, this is how we did relationships.

When I started the journey out of apartheid, I felt apartheid residing deeply in my relationships. I felt disconnected, segregated, separated, apart from others. Then, in 1999, I married a Canadian bartender. Scott loves people. His mom died when he was sixteen, and as awful as that was, in that pain and grief he learned how to be with people—not only in the good things but also in the hard things. I still remember sitting next to him in his little red sports car the day after we'd met. I felt a very strange feeling: I felt at home with him. Not so much in a place as with a person. Three months later we were married. For the next ten years, I watched how he interacted with people, and I learned to relax a little more.

Still, I was hungry for relationship beyond the lines that apartheid had drawn. I felt this hunger in the nooks and crannies of my skin. I was thirty-seven, the mother of three children, and had lived on three continents. I had friends and neighbors from around the world—Dubai, Taiwan, Honduras, India, Trinidad, Sierra Leone. But I still did not have any South African friends who were Black, Indigenous, or People of Color. Not one. There was a deep ache—not just in my heart but also in my body. I longed for South African friends who didn't have white skin and blue eyes. I was hungry for friends who didn't speak the same language, but also friends who did. I was hungry for the end of apartheid in my South African friendships.

When I flew to Kenya in 2010, it was an intentional choice away from whiteness. I wanted to be in a room with people and ideas where whiteness was not at the center. Then René August, a fellow South African and one of the leaders of Amahoro Africa at the time, walked over to me one morning after a session and invited me to breakfast. I kept it very cool on the outside, but on the inside I was jumping with delight.

On that Friday morning, I felt giddy, and I anguished over what to wear. I still remember walking across the lawn of the hotel toward the dining room, my body feeling both anxious and excited. Years before, twelve thousand-plus of my Afrikaner ancestors had made a long journey toward the interior of South Africa, a movement of emigration that came to be known as the Great Trek.[3] It was their act of resistance against British rule in the Cape Province. Instead of submitting to the policies of the British government, they loaded their wagons and headed north, in search of autonomy and pasture.

On that Friday morning in Mombasa, I was making a new kind of Great Trek—a journey across the years and distances that apartheid had laid down between us as fellow South Africans. It was my journey of defiance—refusing to accept the old laws and the rules of apartheid and choosing to weave our lives together in relationship instead.

When René showed up at breakfast, she plopped into the chair across from me and just started talking. She was casual and light-hearted. But because of apartheid, I found myself in unchartered territory. My heart was beating wildly, and my mouth felt dry. Thankfully, René is gracious, wise, and charming.

"Where did you grow up?" she asked.

When I told her, she realized Afrikaans was my mother tongue and immediately switched to Afrikaans.[4] My mind and body froze. My tongue felt thick inside my mouth. Muzzled. I treaded across the landscape between us like it was a minefield. *What if I say the wrong thing?* I wondered.

I was scared to hurt her with my words. I wanted to get it all right, but I didn't know how to move forward. I stuttered over words and stumbled through sentences. I felt like I had rocks in my mouth. I didn't know how to dance with her in Afrikaans. I needed language and didn't have it yet. But I was willing to be awkward as hell. I listened. I watched. I took my cues from her. I learned. I asked about her life, her story, her family. René chatted with me like it was the most ordinary thing to do on a Friday morning. The very fact that it *wasn't* ordinary to me to

have breakfast with this Black friend from South Africa rever-
berated through my entire body.

I grieved for what apartheid had done. I grieved for the relationships Apartheid had stolen from us. I grieved for how
much more it had stolen from Black, Indigenous, and People of
Color. I ached over the long road it would take for the world to
become just and for the paths between our souls to be beautiful,
whole, and straight. I was also ridiculously grateful. Breakfast
that morning meant the end of another apartheid.

● ● ● ● ●

In 2012 Amahoro Africa took place in Burundi on the edge
of Lake Tanganyika. At night we could hear drums from the
Democratic Republic of the Congo in the distance. Kelley had
invited me to participate in a Women's Theological Intensive led
by René and Latin American theologian Ruth Padilla DeBorst.
Amahoro—which means "peace" in Kirundi—had already
been such a place of peace and restoration for me in Kenya. I
couldn't wait to gather with old friends and make new friends.

This time my friend Tina Francis-Mutungu came along.
When we landed in Burundi, both Kelley and Claude were there
to welcome us at the airport. Slowly, beautifully, the distances
I'd felt in my bones for so many years were melting away. Something new was being woven—sisterhood and a large tapestry
of humanity.

On the day the gathering started, I learned that Nicole
Joshua, a Bible teacher from South Africa, would be my room-
mate for the week. Over the next five days, through sleepy
late-night conversations and early morning wake-up calls, we
formed a deep friendship.

Our bungalow on the edge of Lake Tanganyika became a
safe space. As we dared to be brave with each other, our hearts
were woven together.[5] We shared honestly about the past, about
living in South Africa during apartheid. We found common

126

Nicole Joshua was kind enough to write the following statement about her identity, and I wanted you to hear it in her own words:

I am a Coloured woman. *Coloured* is an identification that was created by the apartheid government of South Africa by combining groups of peoples that didn't fit cleanly into the categories Black, White, or Indian. Coloured identity is characterized by erasure (of any hint of Blackness in the family tree) and displacement (from homes and neighborhoods that were declared as being for Whites only) that resulted in trauma for those who first experienced it and generational trauma for their children and grandchildren.

Families were torn apart as some were classified as white and others were classified as Coloured using ridiculous tests such as the pencil test. (If a pencil passed unhindered through your hair, you were considered white.) Many people within our communities, especially during apartheid, refused the classification of Coloured, and claimed Black as a self-identification.

Many of us proudly claim the designation Coloured. It is an identification that is still in the making as we work to reclaim those aspects of us that were erased. Aspects such as honoring, recognizing, and reclaiming the identity, cultures, and languages of the Indigenous peoples of the Western Cape that were subsumed and effectively erased under the category "Coloured"; reclaiming the parts of our family tree that are descended from enslaved people; celebrating foods that grew out of our communities such as *gatsbys* (a long bread roll filled with meats, hot chips, and salad, big enough to feed four people) and pickled fish; reclaiming the root of Afrikaans, known as *Afrikaaps,* with its first dictionary being published; and celebrating our humor, stories, language, food, and communities.

ground in our love for Jesus, God's people, good theology, and laughter.

What started in our pajamas became a friendship that has brought our families together across different continents. I am so grateful that we get to weave a new story.

● ● ● ● ●

While I was writing this chapter, the news was filled with the deaths of six Asian American women who were murdered by a white supremacist in Atlanta, Georgia.[6] That man, the son of a Baptist preacher and a baptized member of the Southern Baptist Convention, walked into three different spas and opened fire. He killed eight people.

In 2020 police officers broke down the door of Breonna Taylor's apartment in Louisville, Kentucky, and killed her while she was in bed.[7]

The spaces between us are not benign. They are filled with stories and histories, laws and deceit, sermons and stereotypes, news headlines and family members going missing and being murdered. They are filled with anger, fear, hatred, grief, loss, distrust, and so much more. The spaces between us are not empty.

In episode 6 of the video web series *The Next Question*, Austin Channing Brown shares an image of the distances between us.[8] She quotes an excerpt from the film *The Color of Fear (Part 2)*, saying, "I need you to know that every time I form a relationship with another white person, I'm crawling on my hands and knees over the broken shards of other relationships where I was betrayed."[9]

I have been pausing on those words for a very long time.

My white body is not yet a safe place for Black, Indigenous, and People of Color. It's not about whether I believe it to be a safe space but whether it's *experienced* as a safe space by Black, Indigenous, and People of Color. I cannot assume that because

I have good intentions or even show up for anti-racism work, my body and presence will be welcomed. White bodies have a long, global history of inflicting harm. Otegha Uwagba writes, "White people are eroding my body."[10] The sociological term is *weathering*, describing "how the chronic stress of constant exposure to racism negatively impacts Black people's health."[11] Our good intentions are not enough. In fact, our good intentions can often be harmful.

That image of the shards of glass lining the distances between us breaks my heart. It also compels me to do the work of picking up the shards between us, piece by broken piece, and not adding any new shards. There are no to-do lists or checklists for earning trust. But I know this: I don't want any of my human siblings to suffer and walk across a path lined with glass shards.

So, I check in: Have I done anything to betray someone's trust today? Have I done anything that may have harmed or diminished someone along my path today? If so, did I ask, "How may I restore you?" Did I apologize when I made a mistake? Did I relinquish my desire for forgiveness when I did the wrong thing?

I can also reflect on my physical presence. Did I listen well? Was I mindful of how much space I took up in a meeting or in a room? Was I aware of who spoke up and who didn't? Did I speak up when someone made a racist or violent remark? Did I pick up on any microaggressions? Did I do something about it?

Then I also ask whether I practiced self-compassion. I remember that if my compassion does not extend to myself, I will not be able to sustain this work.

Picking up the shards between us is about valuing a person enough to *want* to earn their trust. To want to make things right. Not just in our personal interactions but also in the collective realm. I cannot alleviate the suffering of all, but I can do my part today. It is time to remove the glass from the spaces between us and gently, faithfully earn the trust that is needed to build relationships for a different world.

Station of Relationship

Recovering from our internalized racism takes place in a web of relationship. I have a blue ceramic container in my office where I place what I call my objects of re-membering. Consider creating a container for your own objects of re-membering. Along this path, not only do we need reminders of the pain racism has caused; we are also being put together in a new way as we walk the path of the recovering racist. I have gathered three large shards from a broken vase and placed them in the area where I light my candles. They remind me of Austin Channing Brown's words—the pain of broken promises and broken relationships. They remind me of the work that is required to remove the broken glass from our world.

"Nearly all of our bodies—bodies of all culture—are infected by the virus of white-body supremacy [WBS]," writes trauma specialist Resmaa Menakem.[12] To get rid of this virus, Menakem is creating a movement for somatic abolitionism. Somatic abolitionism "heals our bodies of the WBS virus, and then inoculates our bodies against new WBS infections through cultural container building. It begins in your body, then ripples out to other bodies, and then to our collective body."[13]

Showing up for somatic abolition, I am mindful of how much work lies ahead in my own body as well as in our collective body of humanity. But I am committed to being part of building a different cultural container and a different world. I want my white body to do less harm, inflict less pain, and become a safe place for other bodies. I am committed to the web of relationship we call humanity. What about you?

▷ REFLECT

- If it is safe or comfortable for you to do so, find a broken shard, hold it in your hand, and let it speak to you. What do you need to hear about broken relationships? Turn your reflections into a prayer. Write it down or share it with a recovering racist friend.

- Reflect on your white body and how it shows up in a room. How will you make your white body a safe body for Black, Indigenous, and People of Color? Consider joining a course like Resmaa Menakem's somatic abolition course.[14] What else is available to you?

- Where have you been invited into relationships of peace? How can you honor those relationships today?

The journey of the recovering racist is a journey of relationship.

12

HONORING EVERYONE

Dignity is different from respect. Dignity is a birthright. We have little trouble seeing this when a child is born; there is no question about children's value and worth. If only we could hold onto this truth about human beings as they grow into adults. . . . Treating others with dignity, then, becomes the baseline for our interactions. We must treat others as if they matter, as if they are worthy of care and attention.

—Donna Hicks[1]

If one member suffers, all the members suffer with it; if one member is honored, all the members share its joy.

—1 Corinthians 12:26 IB

Flip was an elderly man, a Person of Color, who occasionally worked in our garden when I was a young girl. He carefully trimmed the edges of our kikuyu lawn by hand. I remember him sitting on his haunches, slowly moving about the edges of our garden.

In Afrikaner culture, respect for the elderly is imperative. We call any authority figure by a title. Anyone who is older and wiser—a teacher, an uncle, an aunt, anyone who seems old enough to deserve respect—is addressed by a title such as *Oom*, meaning "Uncle," or *Tannie*, meaning "Aunt."

For as long as I can remember, Flip was always called Flip. I never called him Uncle or Sir. I called him Flip, like he was an equal. I was a pip-squeak of a child who wore ribbons in her ponytails. He was an elder. Ma kept his enamel plate, his mug, his fork, and his spoon underneath the sink in the kitchen. His plate lived next to the dishwashing liquid and the extra dish-cloths, by the Sunlight soap and the scrub brushes. Apartheid lived in that cupboard.

When I became friends with Kelley Nikondeha, I learned about the Batwa people, who had historically been marginal-ized in Burundi. During my first visit to Burundi, we hung out in Kelley and Claude's living room one afternoon. She explained to us the hierarchies that existed in Burundi.

"When Batwa people are invited to a wedding in Burundi," she said, "they usually have to sit at a separate table. At wed-dings, their cups and plates, their knives and forks are washed separately. Sometimes caterers don't even bother washing their dishes separately. They just smash all the dishes the Batwa people ate from. Nothing can touch."

I gasped.

Later, while we were standing in the kitchen, I asked her about the cups and the plates, the knives and the forks. Was it true about the Batwa people at weddings? Did I hear that correctly?

She nodded.

I thought of Flip's cup and plate and spoon and fork, so care-fully kept underneath our kitchen sink. We had done the same.

* * * * *

This cup is the new covenant in my blood; do this, whenever you drink it, in remembrance of me.

—1 Corinthians 11:25

A few days later, a group of us piled into a truck and drove out into the hills outside Bujumbura to the community of Matara, where Kelley and Claude first began their development work with the Batwa people. We walked up into the hills, through coffee and banana plantations, rows of sugar cane and corn wrapped up in humid air. It was green and lush as far as the eye could see. Beautiful rows of food, of life, of work, of dignity. It smelled like heaven.

At the top of a steep climb, we were shown to an open-air hut with a thatched roof, where we sat down with the community leaders. Their leathered brown skin reminded me of Flip's skin.

I couldn't help wondering what it could have been like if Flip had been given his own parcel of land, tools, and support. What could he have accomplished? What if he had been given the opportunity to grow his own garden, walk in dignity, and not eat from the hand of a white person?

I listened to stories that day and let healing wash over me. The healing of the unspoken superiority so instilled in me, so deeply embedded in my soul. I listened as wise leaders in that community spoke with dignity and pride. I let their Black pride seep into the deepest parts of me, deep into the roots of white superiority lies.

Somebody had carried a big yellow crate up into the hills and offered us bottles of Fanta. I sat down on the floor next to one of the female leaders in the community and slipped out of my shoes. Barefoot, seated on the bare earth, I wanted to honor the land and her people. I wanted to honor the people I had been invited to share a bottle of Fanta with. This was holy ground. Deep within, I was becoming whole.

When Jesus entered into my shame story, he said, "Gather up the leftovers so nothing will be wasted" (see John 6:12).

"Bring me the fragments of your story, because they can have purpose." I began to bring Jesus the story of Flip and his cup and his plate and his spoon and his fork. I opened the bottom cupboard in my childhood kitchen and reached into the pain and the shame. I looked at the cup and the plate and the spoon and the fork for a long time, because I did not remember them lightly. Then I brought them to Jesus and said, "See, Lord? See this cup? See this plate? This spoon? Here's the evidence of how I have betrayed you and your beloved humanity. I have separated us."

And this is what I sensed him say:

Drink from the cup of forgiveness, my daughter.
Drink from the cup of redemption, my daughter.
Drink from the cup of freedom.
It is for freedom that I have set you free.

So, when we lifted our Fanta bottles to our thirsty lips that day in Matara, it was Communion. I drank like it was the blood of Jesus, because sitting there on that cool Burundian earth, it was like I was sitting with Flip and his friends. I *was* having Communion. I was with Jesus and Flip and these Batwa friends in a hut in the hills of Matara, but this time I had eyes to see the full and beautiful circle of humanity.

Apartheid had taught me to disrespect. Love has taught me to honor.

● ● ● ● ●

In February 2012, I hopped into a minivan with several friends and drove down to Portland, Oregon, for the Justice Conference. One of the people I was most excited to hear from was Miroslav Volf, the Croatian theologian who teaches at Yale and who has written several books, including *Exclusion and Embrace*.

Volf preached a compelling message on these two words: honor everyone. The message was based on 1 Peter 2:16–17: "Live as free people, but don't hide behind your freedom when you do evil. Instead, use your freedom to serve God. Honor everyone. Love your brothers and sisters in the faith. Fear God" (GW). Volf said, "'Honor'—not merely 'don't demean' or 'tolerate,' but honor. And 'everyone'—not only 'those in our political camp' or 'with our moral persuasions,' but everyone." Then Volf asked, "If Christ calls us to honor everyone, who would you have a hard time honoring?"[2]

My heart sank. It wasn't the people I had been taught to dishonor. It wasn't the people who had been dishonored by the laws and the systems of oppression in South Africa. For me, the people hardest to honor were those who had racist ideas and racist behaviors. When Volf asked that question, an image came to mind almost immediately. It was a stereotypical image depicting a conservative Afrikaner, known as a Boer. (It literally means "farmer.") At their extreme, Boers were members of the Afrikaner Resistance Movement[3] in South Africa, people who advocate for a separate white state.

Thud. I had not expected that.

I knew this was something I had to wrestle with. Psychologists call this the shadow self. According to Carl Jung, the shadow self is the person we would rather not be.[4] "Jung first gave us the term 'shadow' to refer to those parts of our personality that have been rejected out of fear, ignorance, shame, or lack of love."[5] We must face the darkness within ourselves in order to bring it into light.

If we deny our racism, we also suppress the opportunity to dismantle it and heal it within. If we deny our racism, we are still attached to the myth of white supremacy. If we deny our racism, we let shame, guilt, fear, or something else have the power. If we deny our racism, we cannot be authentic, whole allies in dismantling racist systems in our world. We still want to be in the center of the story, abuse power, or flex our goodness. It is still about us rather than about simply taking our place in the larger story of love, seeking justice and weaving a new world.

"Be willing to find out that you 'are' what you least want to be," writes Debbie Ford in *The Dark Side of the Light Chasers*.[6] She wrote that book in 1998—a deep dive into our shadow selves—and acknowledged that she was racist, one of the things she, too, least wanted to be. "Unconcealing is the first step of the shadow process," she says. "Unconcealing requires rigorous honesty and willingness to see what you hadn't been able to see. Acknowledgment of our shadow self begins the process of integration and healing."[7]

I felt deeply challenged. The message of Jesus calls me to love everyone. When the person I least wanted to honor was a racist stereotype, I realized that person represents a part of me. I belong to that person too. I have come to understand that this image represents a part of myself that I did not want to see. To love the person I would rather not honor is also to love myself. To love the person I would rather dismiss, despise, or reject is to speak grace to the deep divide between us as humans. To love someone I see as an Other is to love and honor my enemy. To love my enemy is to love the parts of me that feel least deserving. I am called to honor everyone.

This journey of recovering from internalized racism both heals us and saves us. What is so shattered between us as humans can be healed in us and through us. Recovering racists do the work to honor everyone.

Station of Honoring

As we pause here at the station of honoring, let's reflect on the idea of honor. It holds a breadth of meaning: to esteem, to hold in high regard, to respect. It speaks of relationship and how we value one another. Remember how systems have been set up to dishonor, harm, diminish, and dehumanize Black, Indigenous, and People of Color.

What would be, for you, a posture of honor? Take that posture of honor—against the forces that have worked to dishonor for so many centuries—and do it as a small act of resistance.

As I move in the world, I like to practice "small acts of honor" throughout the day, acknowledging my existence in the large web of humanity. A small act of honor acknowledges our shared humanity and the dignity in each and every person. Small acts of honor acknowledge that there's room for everyone in the circle, allowing someone else to go first, offering kindness. Ashlee Eiland writes, "Kindness may be a mushy word, but it's the dark horse of our humanity. It's not loud or demanding, but given enough time, it wins."[8] What small acts of honor can you think of?

Robin Wall Kimmerer, Potawatomi citizen, scientist, and author of *Braiding Sweetgrass* writes, "We need acts of restoration, not only for polluted waters and degraded lands, but also for our relationship to the world." She says that "we need to restore honor to the way we live, so that when we walk through the world we don't have to avert our eyes with shame, so that we can hold our heads up high and receive the respectful acknowledgment of the rest of the earth's beings."[9]

Today I also want to honor you. I honor you for doing this work, for caring, for showing up. I see your humanity, and I am reminded of your belovedness. I honor you, right where you are today.

If you are comfortable, place your hand on your heart. What does honor feel like in your body? In your heart? What would it feel like to walk through the world in healed and whole relationship with the world? Let's keep working on honoring everyone.

▷ **REFLECT**

A special word to victims of violence and abuse. In this context, the questions below apply to our place in the story of racism, not to our place as victims of abuse. I honor your healing journey and the work you are doing to honor yourself. I honor the woman who rose inside me and said, "Enough." May you be gentle with yourself. I honor your journey, wherever you are.

- What does honor mean to you?
- When have you felt honored? When have you felt dishonored?
- Who have you not honored?
- Who would be the hardest person(s) for you to honor? Why? What do they represent to you?
- What can you do today to practice honoring everyone?
- What one small act of honor can you practice today?

The journey of the recovering racist is a journey of honoring everyone.

PART 5
REPAIR

Practice of Liberation: Nourishing the Soul

Padkos means "food for the road" in Afrikaans. You can find cement tables all along the main highways of South Africa for people to pull over and eat padkos.

My mom used to make *frikkadelle*—meatballs hand-rolled with ground beef, breadcrumbs, milk, and egg. I loved apricot jam and cheese sandwiches, and we would always have boiled eggs. She made sweet coffee with milk and poured it into a flask the morning right before we left. This was our padkos, and it always felt like a treat, like soul nourishment, as much as it was feeding our bodies.

When I think of padkos, I can still feel wind whipping against my face from cars or trucks passing by on the lonely highway in the Karoo. I can still hear birds singing. As a young girl, I often watched the insects, like giant ants or a toktokkie beetle, scurry about my feet. They reminded me to slow down.

As we take this journey together, remember to pause, eat your padkos, and nourish your body, soul, and spirit along the way. Pack your padkos basket with items that remind you of the goodness of life and humanity.

▷ REFLECT

- What's in your padkos basket?
- How will you remind yourself of your humanity—and the humanity of everyone we serve—as you do the work of anti-racism?
- What beautiful and good things nourish your soul?
- Take time to partake of some padkos.

On the journey of the recovering racist,
we take time to nourish body and soul.

13

KNITTED TOGETHER

Do the best you can until you know better.
Then when you know better, do better.

—Maya Angelou[1]

Michael Lapsley was born in New Zealand and is an Anglican priest and social justice activist who became one of the victims of political violence in the struggle for a democratic South Africa. In 1990, a letter bomb exploded as he opened it. He lost both hands and an eye, and both eardrums were shattered.[2]

These days Lapsley runs the Institute for Healing of Memories[3] in Cape Town, helping people move from destructive memory to life-giving memory. "I believe the time for Healing of Memories has come in the human family," he says. "In the wake of wars and strife there have to be just settlements of the political and economic issues that divide us, but complementary to these we must address the psychological, emotional and spiritual aftermath of conflicts." He adds, "Unless we bind up the wounds of the broken-hearted, we cannot hope to create a just and durable society where everyone has a place in the sun, for the victims of the past too easily become the victimizers of the future. . . . Disability has taught me that we need each other to be fully human, and we can be healers of one another."[4]

● ● ● ● ●

Dr. Rachel Naomi Remen, author of *My Grandfather's Blessings*, shares a beautiful story called "The Birthday of the World."[5] It is an ancient story her grandfather, a rabbi, told her growing up. The story goes something like this.

In the beginning, there was a holy darkness called the Ein Sof. It was the source of life, and at a moment in history, "the world of a thousand things emerged from the heart of the holy darkness as a great ray of light."[6]

But then there was an accident. All the vessels that contained the light of the world broke, and the wholeness of the world—the light of the world—scattered. It was broken into a thousand pieces. The fragments of light fell into everyone and everything—into all people, into all events, and over all time. To this day, there is a hidden fragment of the light of the world in every person and every event. When we gather the fragments together, we become the wholeness of the world.

"We are here," says Remen, "because we are born with the capacity to find the hidden light in all events and all people; to lift it up and make it visible once again and, thereby, to restore the innate wholeness of the world."[7] This task is called *tikkun olam* in Hebrew—the restoration, or repair, of the world. "I think that we all feel that we're not enough to make a difference—that we need to be more, somehow, either wealthier or more educated or, somehow or other, different than the people we are. And according to this story, we are exactly what's needed. And to just wonder about that a little, what if we were exactly what's needed? What then? How would I live if I was exactly what's needed to heal the world?"[8]

How would you and I live if we were exactly what's needed to heal the world?

• • • • •

In January 2016, I was invited to participate in a weeklong gathering on Robben Island off the coast of Cape Town. Twelve years earlier, I had fallen to my knees in that same place. Only God had heard my cries of repentance, my pleas for justice and forgiveness, my longing for a different story for our country. I'd told nobody except Scott and my journal. Twelve years later, I was on my way to participate in a global gathering with faith leaders who would ask, "What does Jesus have to do with justice?"

When I landed in London's Heathrow Airport early Friday morning, I found an airport chair and pulled up my feet, my journal, and my Bible. I had a long layover on my way to Cape Town, and I wanted to get my heart ready. *Was there anything I needed to be mindful of? Did God have anything to say to me?* The question that kept coming to my heart was this: *What do you hope to find there, Idelette?*

I felt compelled to open my Bible to that familiar text in Psalm 139. *Interesting*, I thought. *Why Psalm 139 now, God?*

I'd read that psalm many times. I'd always read it and heard it preached as God caring so personally for each of us as individuals. How intentionally and carefully God knits our being together in our mother's womb. It is a psalm that reminds us of our belovedness. It is a psalm that speaks of God's tender intentionality. But, for me, it had always been an individual reading.

That Friday morning, the psalm took on new meaning. I was on my way to the Mother City,[9] the city we also call Cape Town, in my motherland. I thought of God as Mother, like a hen who gathers her chicks under her wings (Matt. 23:37). I thought about how a mother hen would want to keep her chickens safe—safe from the violence in our world. I thought about the violence against Black bodies, in particular, and about the deaths of Freddie Gray, Eric Garner, Tamir Rice, Michael Brown, Sandra Bland, and so many other people.[10] I thought of the painful, fragmented state of humanity.

So with my Bible on my lap open to Psalm 139 and mindful of my departure to the Mother City in a few hours, I began reading.

This knitting together is not just for me, I thought. *It's for us.*

In a cold and bare airport waiting room, under fluorescent lights, I read Psalm 139 as God knitting us, as humanity, together again. And then I prayed it as a prayer, thinking of all the fragments, the ways we have harmed each other, and the damage white supremacy has done:

> Knit us together, God.
> We are so complex, but you are good for making us
>   complex.
> Knit us together, O God,
> knit us together.
> Where and when we have been ripped apart,
> pick up the threads of our souls
> and knit us together.
> Knit us together in the womb
> of our Mother.
> We have been an unraveled people . . .
> we have been ripped apart
> and torn each other to shreds.
> Knit us together, Holy One.
> Knit us together.
> Thank you for making us so wonderfully complex.
> Your workmanship is marvelous. . . .
> Forgive us when we have not honored
> the dignity of each person,
> the worth of each human being,
> when we have not had eyes to see
> how marvelous it is to behold another one of your
>   children.

Knit us together, Holy One.
Knit us together.

As God's creation, knitted together in our Mother's womb, we are magnificent. Our knitted-togetherness—our belonging to each other—is beautiful. We were always meant to be glorious together.

We are not there yet. But this is the longing of my heart. There is work to do.

●　●　●　●　●

In John 6, we read the story of Jesus feeding the large crowd. It's a story of miraculous provision, but it's also a story about fragments. *After* the miracle, Jesus tells the disciples, "Gather up the leftover pieces so that nothing gets wasted" (John 6:12 IB). The King James Version says, "Gather up the fragments that remain, that nothing be lost."

Jesus cares about the broken bits, the fragments. Jesus cares about the broken shards of our stories—the pieces that others would throw away or dismiss. Jesus cares about the shards lining the paths between us. Jesus says, "Gather up those fragments. Don't let them be wasted." Jesus cares about the fragments of our human story. Let the heart of God remind us: all these fragments have value. God is doing the knitting together, and we have been invited to join the work.

Our violence toward each other—in word and in deed—has ripped us apart in so many ways. The word *religion* comes from the Latin word *religare*, meaning "to bind up." Religion reconnects us. Walking with God and practicing the ways of God are meant to reconnect us and bind us together, to God and to each other. It is time for the fragments to be gathered. It is time to become knit together, as humanity, in Mother God's womb.

Birth us anew, Lord.
Remake us as humanity.

Station of Knitting Together

Confronting our internalized racism is a shattering. It is a coming to the end of ourselves and allowing the Spirit to gather us and make us whole in a new way. Find an object that safely represents to you the brokenness in our world. Can you imagine this object as part of a much larger wholeness?

The Spirit gathers us as individuals—one stitch, one heart, one body at a time. But there is also a collective gathering and healing taking place—a healing of the body of the world. Every time we take a step towards healing the violence between us and restoring relationship, we are remaking the world. We participate in the knitting together of the world. Kelley Nikondeha writes, "Our small gestures insist that everyone belongs and that the structures of the world must be calibrated towards inclusion."[11]

If you feel comfortable, write your own prayer for the healing of the world. May we join in what the Spirit is already doing.

▷ **REFLECT**

- How can you be a part of the knitting together of the world?
- What would it mean for you to see the light in every person, in every broken shard in our world?
- What would it mean for you to see your own light as part of this world?
- Whose light can you make visible today?
- What small action can you take to repair our world today?

On the journey of the recovering racist, we become part of God's work of knitting us together as humanity.

14

CONTENDING FOR PEACE

If we have no peace, it is because we have forgotten that we belong to each other.

—Mother Teresa[1]

"I am not allowed to go on this next road," said Hussain, our Palestinian tour guide. "It is illegal for Palestinian people to walk here."

We were about to round the corner to Shuhada Street in Old Hebron.

In November 2016, I was with a group of North American women, learning how to be everyday peacemakers with the Global Immersion Project.[2] When our bus stopped outside the Tomb of the Patriarchs that morning, the air felt particularly heavy. I noticed the presence of Israeli soldiers—more than at any other place we'd visited—and I learned that there are between 600 and 650 soldiers for every Jewish settler in Hebron.[3]

As we walked slowly, quietly down Shuhada Street, we noticed that the doors of all the homes and shops facing the street had been welded shut. There is no entry from this street.

Palestinian people who still live on Shuhada Street have to enter their own homes via back doors or rooftops. They are not allowed on this street.

Years before, I'd heard the occupation of Palestine called an apartheid.[4] It was why I was there—my story requiring me to pay attention whenever I learned about another apartheid in our world. Walking down Shuhada Street, I breathed it again, smelling it, tasting it, feeling the oppression in my body. Two worlds converging. I thought of the forced removal of communities in South Africa. I thought of the silence imposed on Robert Sobukwe on Robben Island. I thought of the signs keeping Black, Indigenous, and People of Color from entering the movie theater or public pool in our town.[5] While the military presence, the welded-shut doors, the barbed wire, and the propaganda yelled loudly from the streets, this time I had eyes to see and ears to hear who was not there. Apartheid was alive and well in Hebron.

When we met up with Hussain again, he led us to the mandatory checkpoint for all Palestinian people. In Hebron, Palestinian residents have to walk through this checkpoint every time they leave the house, even for something as simple as going to the grocery store. I watched a Palestinian mom with two young boys navigate the checkpoint ahead of us. These boys are growing up with Israeli soldiers on every corner monitoring their every move. Every time they pass through the checkpoint, they are at the mercy of the soldiers.

"The turnstile at the checkpoint has the same name as the machine that plucks chickens at the butcher," Hussain told us. "Sometimes soldiers yell out that name as we go through the turnstile. Every time we are reminded of being plucked of our dignity and our humanity." It was a violence to the soul.

As we walked through the nearly deserted marketplace, we saw a few traditional Palestinian women's dresses—in red and black, but mostly red—hanging from the ceiling. Most storefronts were locked up and shut tight. Not too much for sale here. The sense of abandonment in the market and the dresses, hanging in the silence, connected my heart to yet another injustice. Standing in Old Hebron, I was reminded of the REDress Project,[6] an art installation that tells the story of missing and murdered Indigenous women and girls in Canada.[7]

As we walked through the streets of Hebron, it was difficult not to choose sides. It would have been easy to feel indignant, angry, and riled up. But I was reminded of the words—a warning, really—I had heard from an Israeli peacemaker before I'd left Canada: "If you have come here to choose sides, don't bother. Go home. But if you have come here to help us figure this out, if you have come here to help us find the way of peace, then we welcome you."

Choosing to contend for peace felt like dropping into a deeper place in my humanity. It felt like walking through yet another door—one that would be costly but one that would invite me even closer into the heart of love.

I thought of Archbishop Emeritus Desmond Tutu, who, in spite of the dehumanization of apartheid, kept choosing to make peace. I thought of President Nelson Mandela, who had spent twenty-seven years in prison and yet chose peace. I thought of Malala Yousafzai, who keeps contending for peace. I thought of survivors of residential schools in Canada, people like Chief Dr. Robert Joseph, who keep choosing to make peace.

These global heroes intentionally choose to love their enemies. My journey of recovering from internalized racism was now saying, "It's time to learn the way of peace."

* * * * *

Moira and Rami sat on two chairs next to each other at the front of the room. They were representatives of the Parents Circle–Families Forum (PCFF), a joint Israeli-Palestinian peace organization of over six hundred families.[8] Each of these families had lost a loved one to the conflict. Each of these families had chosen to tell their story and walk toward their enemies. I watched as Moira and Rami chatted with each other before we started. They seemed relaxed in each other's company.

Moira Jilani had lost her Palestinian husband in 2010 when Israeli police fired three bullets at him point-blank on the streets of Jerusalem.[9] Zaid, her husband, lay there for twenty minutes before he died. Nobody helped him. His death had filled Moira with anger and pain. A representative from PCFF came to visit her and told Moira about her brother's death at the hands of the Israeli Defense Force. Moira didn't understand why this woman didn't want revenge, so she decided to check out the work of PCFF.

It was Rami's story that helped Moira move forward and choose peacemaking.[10] Rami, an Israeli dad, had lost his daughter to a Palestinian suicide bomber in Jerusalem in 1997. Listening to Rami recount the pain and the loss he felt after his daughter's death, Moira understood: "Our pain is the same pain." Society had turned Moira and Rami into enemies. But their shared pain had brought them together. Both chose to become peacemakers.

As I listened to them share, it was clear the pain was still there. But watching these former enemies sitting side by side, forging peace by sharing their stories, felt like an indictment. If these two people could choose peace, how dare I not do the same?

Day after day, as we traveled through Israel and Palestine, we met more local peacemakers. Here, in the heart of their conflict, we met people choosing to walk toward enemies daily.

● ● ● ● ●

Sami Awad, a Palestinian Christian and founder of Holy Land Trust, embodies the lengths someone would go to in their commitment to peace.[11] I first met Sami at a conference in Denver called Simply Jesus, where we were both speakers. Then again when we spent that week on Robben Island in 2016 as part of a global conversation about Jesus and justice. I'd heard him tell his story, but hearing him tell that story again, while standing in Bethlehem, shone a whole new light on his deep commitment to peace.

We had just driven through a military checkpoint to get into Bethlehem. We had seen the inch-by-inch proliferation of Jewish settlements on the hills. We had caught a glimpse of how difficult daily life is for a Palestinian person—limited access to water, daily intimidation and time constraints of passing through checkpoints, and so much more. It was a lot to comprehend, let alone live. And yet Sami stood in front of us and told us of his commitment to peace, following in the footsteps of Jesus.

But there was even more. Years before, his commitment to peace compelled Sami to do something very specific. He decided that to better understand the pain of Jewish people and the roots of Zionism, he needed to travel to Auschwitz. Sami took his body to the place of his enemy's deepest pain. Imagine how costly that was for him. Sami put himself in the shoes of his enemy and immersed himself in their story.

⁕ ⁕ ⁕ ⁕ ⁕

We arrived in Sderot just before sunset and stood with Roni Keidar,[12] a Jewish mother and grandmother, on the beach in her hometown. Out in the distance, behind a huge wall, we could see Gaza.

The Gaza Strip is a small, self-governing Palestinian territory on the eastern coast of the Mediterranean Sea. Many have called it the world's largest open-air prison.[13] Gaza has a population of about two million people who struggle daily to survive, living behind a blockade where access to food, medical supplies, and daily necessities is severely restricted. Power is out for most of the day, and 98 percent of the water in Gaza is contaminated and undrinkable.[14]

Roni took us to a part of the separation wall, stretching more than twenty feet into the sky, where peacemakers had decorated the concrete with messages of hope and peace.[15]

"It's beautiful," we said naively.

Roni shook her head, her face sober. She would rather that separation wall did not exist. Roni's community, right on the border with Gaza, has been deeply affected by rockets, missiles, and bombings. Every bus stop in town has an underground bomb shelter.

"There are too many deaths," she said. Her kids and grandkids have grown up with violence. There is not a family in town that has not been affected.

Years before, Roni had decided that the way forward was not to treat her Palestinian neighbors as enemies but to get to know them instead. So she started contending for peace. She simply started showing up with her car at the checkpoint. She knew that every Palestinian person in Gaza entering into Israel had to go through the checkpoint. So she went there and offered people rides—to doctor's appointments, to checkups, to university interviews. She met them at their place of need, and over time she started building relationship and trust.

Roni shows up for her neighbors in Gaza. They call each other when a rocket or a missile goes off. They check in on each other. Roni Keidar is waging peace in one of the most divided places in our world. She is building bridges, not walls. Through friendship, she is writing a different story.

●　●　●　●　●

Former white nationalist Derek Black is someone I could have loved to despise. But it was in the transformation of his heart that I learned a lot about peacemaking.

Derek Black was born to Don Black, the founder of the world's largest white pride website, Stormfront. Black is also the godson of David Duke, a former grand wizard of the Ku Klux Klan. By the time Derek Black went to college in Sarasota, Florida, he was hosting his own political radio show five days a week while helping moderate Stormfront.[16] When Black's identity became known on campus, students asked, "How do we as a community respond to this?" Was it better to shame or demonize Derek? Or was it more effective to reach out to him?[17] The issue quickly caused an ideological rift.

At a time when Black was ostracized and rejected by most students, two Jewish students invited him to their Friday night Shabbat dinner. Matthew Stevenson, the only Orthodox Jew on campus, knew what it was like to be excluded. He had "already experienced enough shaming at New College to believe that exclusion only reinforced divides."[18] He also knew that Black could stand his ground in any argument. Stevenson decided to try friendship instead. "The goal was really just to make Jews more human for him," Stevenson said.[19] Over time, the two men built mutual respect.

Black's story is of a long, slow softening of his heart, with many people contributing to his ultimate transformation. People didn't give up on him. When I read his story, I felt deeply convicted by the generosity and hospitality of those two Jewish students as well as the consistent commitment of their friend Allison, who kept sending Black information, statistics, and stories, hoping to transform his ideas. In the end, both inclusion and exclusion shifted Black's beliefs. While some students walked toward their enemy, extending an invitation of friendship and community to Black, others excluded him, forcing the white supremacist to consider how his ideology oppressed others.

Black's story reminds me how each of us has a role in peacemaking. It is a slow story of transforming enemies into friends. We also know this is not how every story ends. When I read Black's story, I realized again how deeply entrenched white nationalist ideas had been during apartheid South Africa. I realized that South Africa—and the white bubble I had grown up in—had been the white nationalist state that Black and the white supremacist community had idealized. I had lived it. Black, Indigenous, and People of Color had paid the price for it. It was no ideal; it was an evil abomination. Reading Black's story compelled me to ask, "Who needs to sit at my dinner table? Who needs an invitation to my table this Friday night?"

● ● ● ● ●

Who are your enemies? Where are the deep lines of division drawn in your life? Where have you built a separation wall?

In the United States, Republicans and Democrats are deeply divided and harsh rhetoric flies between the two groups. There is deep division over LGBTQ2S+[20] inclusion in the church. We see it at our dinner tables, at family gatherings, and especially online. Each group is so sure of their ideas that our words have created an ideological apartheid between us as humans.

Jesus calls us to love each other, including our enemies. Lisa Sharon Harper, author and founder of the Freedom Road Institute, reminds us, "The peace of self is dependent on the peace of the other."[21] Peacemakers—lovers of humanity—like Sami, Moira, Rami, and Roni show us that real peace is deeper than polite acceptance of those who are different. It requires us to see the humanity of our enemies. It requires us not only to want peace but to contend for it.

Over and over again, I heard that the conflict in Israel and Palestine is not necessarily my conflict to take up. Peacemaking should be local. I sensed a sobriety, a consistent reminder that making peace is not some sexy cause to pick up; it is very costly.

When people visited Calcutta to see Mother Teresa's ministry to the poor, she instructed them to find the Calcutta in their own backyard.[22] Her words come to mind when thinking about the calling of a peacemaker—not to go and make peace in faraway places but to find the places of violence, conflict, and division in our own nations, in our own communities.

Where do you live? How can you be a Roni Keidar in your own community? How can you be a Sami Awad? Where are you and I specifically called to make peace?

• • • • •

There right in front of me, etched into a granite plaque, were Jesus's words: "Blessed are the peacemakers, for they will be called children of God." We were in Galilee at the Mount of Beatitudes, where it is said Jesus preached the sermon we find in Matthew 5–7. It was the perfect place to bring a group of everyday peacemakers in the making.

Jesus didn't say, "Blessed are the peacekeepers." Instead, Jesus reminded us that the *makers* of peace are blessed—the ones who create something whole out of fragments and shards, weaving together stories of pain and division. The ones who craft peace out of dropped stitches and holes in the world.

Making peace, by implication, means that there is conflict, a divide—an apartheid—between opposing sides. Making peace is seeing the humanity and dignity of each person, including our enemies. Making peace is choosing love as we walk across the minefield of pain, misunderstanding, hatred, violence, trauma, and conflict. Making peace is choosing love, which exists above and beneath and within everything for *everyone*.

Deep breath.

Let's find the Hebron in our own backyards.

Station of Peace

Reflect on a few of these ways to say "peace" in different languages:

Amahoro (Kirundi)

Ping An (Mandarin)

Salaam (Arabic)

Shalom (Hebrew)

Paix (French)

Isithangami (Zulu)

Uxolo (Xhosa)

Kagiso (Setswana)

Vrede (Afrikaans)

Now imagine the face of your enemy and say "peace" to them and work toward meaning it. If it's easier to say it in a different language first, start there.

On the night we visited the garden of Gethsemane, imagining how Jesus had to wait by himself before going to his death on the cross, we drove to a lookout on the Mount of Olives. Our group felt somber and contemplative. The call to make peace felt harder than we could have imagined. But as the sun was setting and we looked out toward the city of Jerusalem in front of us—beautiful, glorious—the words of Psalm 122:6 came to mind: "Pray for the peace of Jerusalem."

Our group began to pray for peace—not just for Jerusalem but for every city in our world where our hearts felt a connection. We said this prayer out loud that night, speaking it into the air in one of the most divided places in the world:

I pray for the peace of Surrey.

I pray for the peace of Vancouver.

I pray for the peace of Cape Town, Johannesburg, and Bloemfontein.

I pray for the peace of Paarl.

I pray for the peace of Chişinău.

I pray for the peace of Manenberg, Mbekweni, and Khayelitsha.

I pray for the peace of Taipei.

I pray for the peace of Hong Kong.

I pray for the peace of Bujumbura, Xiamen, and Beijing.

I pray for the peace of Hebron.

I pray for the peace of Bethlehem.

I pray for the peace of New York, Seattle, and especially Minneapolis.

I pray for the peace of the city where you live.

As I sit on my chair tonight, I am mindful of the power of our words, connecting peace to our heart for people and places. Our prayers for peace ring out into spaces between us filled with division, hatred, strife, pain, and stories. As we long and work for peace, may the God of peace give us strength to keep extending the invitation, keep immersing ourselves in the stories of our enemies, and keep contending for peace.

Here's a confession for the journey as we become peacemakers:

I stand in an active resistance against hatred, against hierarchy thinking, against apathy, against greed. I stand against deception and manipulation, against ignorance, including my own. I stand against violence. I face injustice with courage. I am inspired by the resistance of those who have gone before. I seek to be filled with goodness. I seek to become a little more healed, a little more whole, so that next time I can speak from love, not hate. I seek love. I will keep seeking love. And I will do my best to keep choosing love.

Let it be so.

▷ REFLECT

- Who is *your* enemy?
- How can you walk toward them?
- Where is your Hebron? Where are you called to contend for peace?
- What city is on your heart? Pray for the peace of that city.

The journey of the recovering racist is a
journey of contending for peace.

15

LISTENING FOR THE TRUTH-TELLERS

Our only chance at dismantling racial injustice is being more curious about its origins than we are worried about our comfort. . . . For only by being truthful about how we got here can we begin to imagine another way.

—Austin Channing Brown[1]

"Did you know they call this an apartheid?"

My body froze.

"Excuse me? What did you say?"

"Did you know they call this an apartheid? The way Canada has treated Indigenous people?"

We were in the basement of the Indigenous Friendship Centre on East Hastings Street in Vancouver. It was a rainy November night, and a roomful of people had shown up to become facilitators of the KAIROS Blanket Exercise,[2] an immersive exercise that invites participants into the history of Indigenous people and settler colonialism in Canada, or Turtle Island as many Indigenous people call it.

I was curious why she'd used the word *apartheid*. *Does she know my story?* I wondered.

She didn't.

I had just returned from a ten-day trip to Israel-Palestine for training in everyday peacemaking with the Global Immersion Project.[3] I had been deeply immersed in the story of a current-day apartheid. Years before, I had decided to pay attention whenever I heard the word *apartheid*. It was one of the reasons I'd felt compelled to go to Israel-Palestine. I'd landed back in Canada two days before. I was jet-lagged, processing what I'd seen and experienced, and also in shock from the results of the 2016 US election. I'd been in Jerusalem that election day and hardly slept. Now I stood in Vancouver, and somebody had used that very same word about Canada. I leaned in.

In 1876 the Canadian government passed the Indian Act, a comprehensive piece of legislation that covered all laws and activities that had to do with Indigenous people.[4] It was the government's way of dealing with what they called "the Indian problem."[5] Their intent was not upliftment or the thriving of the original peoples of the land. The intent was extreme assimilation.

In 1887 Sir John A. McDonald, the first prime minister of Canada, said, "The great aim of our legislation has been to do away with the tribal system and assimilate the Indian people in all respects with other inhabitants of the Dominion, as speedily as they are fit for change."[6] A little over thirty years later, in 1920, Duncan Campbell Scott, the deputy superintendent for Canada's Department of Indian Affairs, repeated this idea: "I want to get rid of the Indian problem. . . . Our objective is to continue until there is not a single Indian in Canada that has not been absorbed into the body politic and there is no Indian question, and no Indian Department."[7]

Sit with the full intent of those words. That is our racism. Don't turn away from this history, even if you are not Canadian.

Stay with it. We are human together, and there is enough evidence to show that the British Empire transferred policies, ideas, and techniques that worked in one colony to other places. How has your nation treated Indigenous people?

"The Indian Act has been described as a form of apartheid, a piece of legislation designed to control and tame the Indigenous population. The act historically outlined every aspect of life for an Indigenous person in Canada," writes Tanya Talaga in *Seven Fallen Feathers: Racism, Death, and Hard Truths in a Northern City*. "It was through the Indian Act that the Canadian government formed policy surrounding residential schools, placed bans on religious ceremonies, restricted access to the courts, limited movement by restricting First Nations people from leaving the reserve without permission from an Indian Agent, and prohibited the formation of political organizations."[8]

Talaga shines light on the roots of the sinister connection between Canada, South Africa and apartheid: "The Indian Act was such a successful piece of legislation for the Canadian government that it was used as a model by white South African legislators when they set up their brutal system of apartheid. These two colonial governments of the British Crown share a dark and racist history."[9]

Pierre Bélanger and Kate Yoon dissect the intricate relationship between South Africa and Canada further: "There is sufficient evidence to suggest and confirm that South African government officials received direct information, influence, and inspiration from Canada and its Native reservation system in conceiving and establishing spatial methods of racial segregation."[10] Thomas Berger—a Canadian lawyer, former leader of the New Democratic Party in British Columbia, and a counsel for the Nisga'a Nation—made a speech in 1966 in which he pulled no punches:

The history of the Indian people for the last century has been the history of the impingement of white civilization upon the

Indian: the Indian was virtually powerless to resist the white civilization; the white community of B.C. adopted a policy of apartheid. This, of course, has already been done in eastern Canada and on the Prairies, but the apartheid policy adopted in B.C. was of a particularly cruel and degrading kind. They began by taking the Indians' land without any surrender and without their consent. Then they herded the Indian people onto Indian reserves. This was nothing more nor less than apartheid, and that is what it still is today.[11]

Apartheid in South Africa. Apartheid in Israel-Palestine. But apartheid in Canada? I didn't want to hear that. Like many others, I'd placed Canada on a pedestal as a peacekeeping, refugee-welcoming nation and an example of multicultural- ism and free healthcare. But history does not lie. The truth will come out.

At the launch of the Truth and Reconciliation Commission in Canada, former governor-general to Canada Michaëlle Jean said, "When the present does not recognize the wrongs of the past, the future takes its revenge. For that reason, we must never, never turn away from the opportunity of confront- ing history together—the opportunity to right a historical wrong."[12]

Listen for the truth-tellers.

* * * * *

As recovering racists, we have to account for how our na- tions have treated Indigenous people. It is a history that has repeated itself—not just in former British colonies but around the world. In fact, I first learned about the unjust treatment of Indigenous people when I became friends with Nancy, an Indig- enous woman in Taipei. She told me stories of disappearances of women and girls and loss of land in Taiwan.[13] She invited me to hear the truth even then.

"It takes seven generations to heal," says an Indigenous friend. It takes seven generations for the effects of trauma to be healed in a community. In Canada we have to listen to the truth about the traumatic legacy of residential schools, the Sixties Scoop, the suicide rate among Indigenous youth, the lack of access to fresh water on reserves, and missing and murdered Indigenous women and girls.[14] The pain is deep and wide and long. At the time of writing this book, there is an ongoing search for and discovery of unmarked graves of Indigenous children on the sites of former residential schools across Canada.

Walter Naveau, acting grand chief of the Nishnawbe Aski Nation (NAN) says, "I hear people say that Canada is the greatest nation, but many choose not to acknowledge this country's true history with Indigenous Peoples and the legacy that continues to this day." He continues, "Canada has moved on from the dark days of the Residential Schools, but our people have not. Many are still grieving, and many cannot grieve until they know what happened to their loved ones—the children who were taken away and never made it home."[15]

If you don't know the history of Indigenous people where you live, it's time to learn. Do your research. Start by learning about the history of the land where you live and researching the practice of land acknowledgment—not as a token gesture but as a meaningful practice.[16] Find books, courses, and podcasts to educate yourself about the history. Don't ask Indigenous people to personally educate you. At the same time, listen to Indigenous people who *are* educating society. Shift your reading, your listening, and your learning.

We have much to acknowledge. We have much to make right. We have much to learn. We have much to unlearn. We have a long walk toward each other. "Truth is taking off the bandage so the wound can really heal," Kaitlin Curtice reminds us.[17] May we listen for the truth-tellers.

Station of Truth

Truth, especially about injustice, often does not live in the main-stream. It gets whispered on the edges, on the margins of the status quo. We are so used to listening to dominance that we often confuse the loudest voice with truth. If we want to hear the truth, we have to listen for the truth-tellers. As recovering racists, we listen to the whispers, the anger, the fragments of stories that come from the edges of society, the tears, and the pain. We also get to listen for the joy, the pride, the resilience, the hope, the wisdom, and the love.[18] We get to be part of am-plifying the voices of truth-tellers.

Jesus said, "If you live according to my teaching, you really are my disciples; then you'll know the truth, and the truth will set you free" (John 8:32 IB). I am done with so-called truths that only benefit some but that are not truly liberative. While hearing the truth isn't always easy or comfortable, truth is also not meant to shatter or diminish anyone. Ultimately truth, like love, liberates.

▷ REFLECT

- Which truth-tellers do you need to listen to?
- Where are there gaps in your listening?
- Which truth is hard for you to hear at the moment?
- Where do you need to lean in?
- Which voices are missing from the society where you live or the communities you are part of?
- How will you make an intentional practice of bringing voices that have been marginalized to the center of your consciousness? Write your intention or share it with a recovering racist friend.

*The journey of the recovering racist is a
journey of listening for the truth-tellers.*

16

DECOLONIZING

You cannot discover lands already inhabited.

—Mark Charles[1]

History is entirely created by the person who tells the story.

—Lin-Manuel Miranda[2]

Tina Curiel-Allen, a Xicana/Boricua poet, writer, and activist says, "To talk about decolonization, people need an understanding of what we are decolonizing from." She says,

Colonization is when a dominant group or system takes over and exploits and extracts from the land and its native peoples. Colonization has taken place all over the globe, through the stealing of lands; the raping of women; the taking of slaves; the breaking of bodies through fighting, labor, imprisonment, and genocide; the stealing of children; the enforcement of religion; the destruction—or attempts to destroy—spiritual ways of life. All of these things have left a psychological, spiritual, and physical imprint on indigenous peoples, and a governmental ruling system that we did not create, that was not made for us. These are the things we need to heal from, where we need to start re-claiming. This is where organizing and decolonizing comes in.[3]

Let's pause. We just listened to the words of a truth-teller. At the center of decolonizing—naming it, shaping it, defining it—are people around the world whose lives and ways were colonized by dominant powers.

My ancestors are mostly Western European. As a recovering racist, my task is to interrogate and break free from the racist ideas and systems I inherited from my colonizing ancestors. From 1492 to 1914, European nations conquered or colonized more than 80 percent of the entire world.[4] These colonizing nations included Spain, Portugal, France, Britain, Germany, and the Netherlands. We can trace our lineage on my dad's side back to 1765 when our forefather arrived in the Cape of Good Hope (now Cape Town) from the Netherlands. The history I was taught in high school was entirely shaped by a colonial perspective. I graduated with an A in that history. I have been in the process of unlearning it ever since.[5]

When speaking to our SheLoves church community in 2020, Cheryl Bear from Nadleh Whut´en First Nation offered this view: "What is decolonizing? It's hearing a different story and changing your mind."[6] When Bear said that, one story in particular came to mind. It was a story I had grown up with that had been deeply entrenched in my cultural consciousness and even our Afrikaner cultural celebration. It wasn't until I moved away from South Africa and started hearing different stories that I could return to that old story. It took me years to re-story that story—to reconstruct new meaning from an old narrative. And it was sparked by homemade cheese crisps.

⬤ ⬤ ⬤ ⬤ ⬤

"I like tradition," said Robyn, my sister-in-law, as she handed the women in our book club a container with homemade cheese crisps—a family recipe. One year she baked us each a loaf of her Scottish nana's soda bread; another year she baked us Grandma's squares with lots of caramel and chocolate. She reminded me how important traditions are to her, and it made me think about the traditions I grew up with.

When I moved to Canada, I had shunned most of my Afrikaner cultural traditions and assimilated to life and culture in North America. My Afrikaner traditions reminded me of being on the wrong side of justice—identity, food, and racist history all blended together. So, instead of combing through for good things, I had unconsciously rejected all of our cultural practices and walked away. But that night Robyn challenged me with her cheese crisps and love for traditions. So I asked in prayer, "What do I keep, God? What do I remember?"

I remembered Christmases at my ouma's house—the same house where a photo of Hendrik Verwoerd, known as the architect of apartheid, hung framed on the wall in the living room. We celebrated the birth of a Savior and endorsed apartheid all in the same room. I remembered sitting around the kitchen table in the afternoon with a mug of milky rooibos tea. I remembered watching my mom flip *pannekoek* (the South African version of crepes) on the first rainy day of the season. I remembered learning to *langarm* (two-step) to concertina music, also around that kitchen table.

Then I began to remember another cultural celebration.

When I was growing up, every year the Afrikaner community in South Africa commemorated the Day of the Vow on December 16.[7] It was a religious public holiday—no stores or theaters were open. The day before this holiday, we always had a special assembly in school, and so one of the memories that came back to me was of marching into that assembly carrying in the (old) South African flag.

The Day of the Vow was a day when Afrikaner people gathered to solemnly remember how a handful of Afrikaners prayed for victory over thousands of Zulu warriors. The vow, translated from Afrikaans, reads as follows:

> We stand here before the Holy God of heaven and earth, to make a vow to Him that, if He will protect us and give our enemy into our hand, we shall keep this day and date every year as a day of thanksgiving like a Sabbath, and that we shall erect a house to His honor wherever it should please Him, and that we will also tell our children that they should share in that with us in memory for future generations. For the honor of His name will be glorified by giving Him the fame and honor for the victory.

Nearly 150 years later the Afrikaner community was still keeping its promise, and I was one of the children taught to remember.

The Battle of Blood River took place on December 16, 1838. It is said that over three thousand Zulu warriors died in battle that day, while only three Afrikaners were wounded.[8] It was called the Battle of Blood River because the river turned red from blood.

The day used to be a proud moment in Afrikaner history—the day it was said that God had heard our prayers and helped the Afrikaner people slay another nation. Some still celebrate it, upholding the vow and rallying people around old nationalistic ideas.

The Day of the Vow nurtured exceptionalism in the hearts of Afrikaner people—the belief that a country or group of people is exceptional or unusual, with the implication that they are superior in some way. It was deeply connected to our sense, as Afrikaner people, of being holy, right, and justified in the eyes of a holy God. On this day we celebrated the idea that God was on the side of the Afrikaners. That day "became a rallying point for Afrikaner nationalism, culture and identity."[9] It was and is racist.

And this exceptionalism wasn't particular to South Africa.[10] Former US president Theodore Roosevelt, in his book *The Winning of the West*, quoted this conflict when he expressed his own racist ideas: "The most ultimately righteous of all wars is a war with savages. . . . American and Indian, Boer and Zulu, Cossack and Tartar, New Zealander and Maori—in each case the victor, horrible though many of his deeds are, has laid deep the foundations for the future greatness of a mighty people."[11]

● ● ● ● ●

In 1995, a year after the first democratic election in South Africa, December 16 became the Day of Reconciliation. It is a day to mark the end of apartheid. Even so, many Afrikaners have not relinquished the deep cultural and spiritual connectedness to the Day of the Vow. The story was so embedded into our consciousness that it's difficult for some to take a step back and see it for what it was.

In the privacy of my office, I have fallen to my knees and repented before God for our racist acts at Blood River. I've also taken the original prayer of my people and turned the words into a prayer of repentance. It was my small act of dissent. My honest act of repentance. I had interrogated an old story and changed my mind.

In January 2016, I stood in a circle on Robben Island right next to Musa Njoko, a Zulu sister. We'd first met in Kenya in 2010. Standing there next to her, I was deeply aware of the Day of the Vow and the years I had participated in thanking God for saving the Afrikaner people and, by implication, for slaughtering my sister's ancestors. I could not deny that part of my story.

But standing there arm in arm, I also knew we were part of writing a new story—a story of our connected humanity, of belonging to each other.

The old story no longer works.

● ● ● ● ●

Stone Mountain is the largest Confederate monument in the United States, and it attracts a huge crowd every year on Independence Day, when fireworks light up the faces of Confederate leaders carved into the mountain. Andre Henry calls it "a Confederate Mount Rushmore."[12] Such a celebration would be like celebrating Freedom Day in South Africa with a mountain carved with the faces of apartheid leaders like H. F. Verwoerd, John Vorster, and P. W. Botha. Unthinkable! But it's not always as easy to see the past through new lenses. I didn't see how painful the Day of the Vow was to my Zulu brothers and sisters until I reflected on its legacy and started seeing it through a new lens.

In South Africa, after apartheid fell, there was a lot of change, including changes to the names of streets and provinces. Cities changed their names. There was a powerful effort to remove names and legacies that were painful and confrontational. But many statues remained.

In Cape Town, the statues of Jan van Riebeeck and his wife still stand. The history I had learned was that van Riebeeck had "founded" South Africa, but, of course, Indigenous people had lived in South Africa for centuries already.[13] Van Riebeeck was the first to establish a Dutch trading base and build a fort to defend the Dutch community's claim to the southernmost part of Africa. This is part of the story of my ancestors. Can I hold both the story of my Dutch ancestry *and* the pain colonization have caused Indigenous people in South Africa? Can I be honest about my ancestry *and* the awful history of enslavement along the African coast?

The journey of the recovering racist is about pulling down all the false images we set up about ourselves, our people, and our history. It is painful to admit that we did wrong, but not as painful as it is for those who have been oppressed by that very history. The recovering racist listens to the stories of those who have been oppressed by history. We don't hold on to tradition for tradition's sake. We find new ways to honor who we are without needing to dishonor anyone else. A different way is possible. Monuments and half-truths are not precious. People are.

Station of Decolonizing

For the recovering racist, the journey of decolonization is a journey of relinquishment. Yes, we will be asked over and over again to let go of old stories so we can make room for new stories, different stories, and write a redemptive story instead.

Decolonizing asks us to listen to different stories and reevaluate what we hold as precious. What is too precious to you still? Is it the statue of a former hero? Is it a specific holiday? Is it the name of a sports team or a sports logo that may be offensive and painful to Indigenous people? What is so precious to you that you don't want a liberation journey to touch it?

As part of my liberation, I wrote a new prayer, begging God's forgiveness for what my people did at Blood River. When you are ready, I invite you to write your own prayer of repentance or relinquishment or to express your desire to decolonize.

▷ REFLECT

- What does decolonization mean to you?
- Who told the stories you hold most dear?
- What do you need to relinquish at this time?

The journey of the recovering racist is a journey of decolonizing.

17

RE-MEMBERING

We live in a society in which Indigenous women are targets of abuse—who go missing and are found murdered—and it is unnoticed by so much of the rest of society.

—Kaitlin Curtice[1]

On a clear winter morning in 2017, I drove a rented Hyundai minivan down De Waal Drive into Cape Town. It is a breathtaking road, with Table Mountain on the left, the city at your feet, and below that, the waters of the Atlantic Ocean. I had driven into Cape Town hundreds of times in my life—but from a different entrance. That day I was in the car with my friends Nicole and René, as well as my three kids, and from that new vantage point, I saw something in a way I'd not seen it before.

"There's District Six," René pointed out.

"Where?" I asked, still driving.

"There, where the green grass is."

"Do you mean the part that looks like undeveloped land?"

"Yes," she said.

"District Six? That's it?"

I didn't realize in all the years I'd heard of District Six that I needed to look for something that was no longer there. Now it was obvious. But I didn't see it until a friend pointed it out. On the surface, it looked like grass, a bit of rubble, some rocks. How much can be hidden by empty space? That space told a painful story of racism, forced removals, economic injustice, and the destruction of an entire community. That empty space was not benign. District Six—by its very absence—was telling a story. In order to see what is not there, we need to listen to the ones who know what and who is missing.

The hiddenness—the erasure of an entire community—had done exactly what it had meant to do. But unless we know the story, we don't know the pain. Unless we have eyes to see, we don't perceive.

In February 1966, P. W. Botha, the minister of community development, officially declared District Six a "whites only" area under the Group Areas Act.[2] Nearly a century before, District Six had been established as the Sixth Municipal District of Cape Town.[3] After World War II, it was a bustling community with a multicultural makeup. White people made up only 1 percent of its population, and yet they were the only ones who would eventually be allowed to stay.

The foot of Table Mountain, with a view toward the ocean, is prime real estate; property prices in the center of Cape Town are sky-high. It doesn't take a lot of imagination to understand why the apartheid government wanted to take that land. While District Six was in the heart of Cape Town—some would say it *was* its heart—the sandy Cape Flats were roughly twenty-five kilometers away, without public transit or amenities. In 1968, the removal of nearly thirty thousand people from District Six started. By 1982, more than sixty thousand people had been relocated to the Cape Flats.

The District Six Museum tells the story of how the apartheid government had tried to erase the memory of District Six.[4] They bulldozed the area and dumped the homes and all their contents into the ocean. But photos, videos, and the memories of people still tell the story. I sat down on the floor in front of an art display. I could see a child's leather shoe, pieces of plates and cups and sugar bowls, a doll shoe. There had been so much life here.

"After they removed the houses, they planted grass over where the old streets used to be," René pointed out. "They took away the memories. They wanted people to forget where they'd lived. They didn't want people to go back to the places where they had grown up and played on the streets. . . . They took away the memories." As we walked through the museum, I was transported back in time. It was a time I didn't want to remember but also a time that is crucial to remember. I wanted my kids to witness the story of District Six too.

Nicole sat down on a bench with a sign that read, "Whites Only / Slegs Blankes." During apartheid, it would have been illegal for her to sit there. It was awful to see my friend—a sister of my heart—sit by that sign and be mindful of how it had discriminated against her and others. Benches at the beach. Benches in the park. Benches in town. My body clenched, re-membering the ways apartheid had excluded and dehumanized.

Then Nicole stuck out her tongue at the sign, and we burst out laughing. I joined her on the bench, and we made faces and stuck out our tongues and gave a middle finger to the whole awful story. We laughed and laughed, and it felt so good to write a new story of love and laughter and friendship.

As we walked away from the museum that day, we talked about the journey of re-membering. How when we remember events and places, we are also re-membered. We are put back together in new ways. How often God told God's people to remember, to build an altar so they could remember how God had showed up.

In District Six, my forefathers had worked to erase the memory of an entire community of people. They had actively worked against the ways of God. Their intent was to erase evidence of humanity, life, and family. God wouldn't have it.

When we walked back out into the street and into the sunny day, I noticed a plaque on the street. I paused to read it:

All who pass by
    Remember with shame the many thousands of people who lived for generations in District Six and other parts of this city, and were forced by law to leave their homes because of the colour of their skins.
    Father, forgive us . . .

I paused and I prayed those words. I re-membered.

To dismember is to tear apart. When we re-member, we are putting things back together: fragments, stories, memories, communities. We join the Spirit's work of knitting us together. The fragments that have been scattered and the pieces of our humanity that have been sacrificed on altars of dehumanization and greed are slowly returned to us.

On the journey of dismantling our inner racism, what is the task for white people? So often, stories like the story of District Six don't live at the center. They are not validated by the center of power because they were erased by those who held power. For example, P. W. Botha was respected in our home. He proclaimed he was a Christian, a member of the Dutch Reformed Church, and what he said was regarded as right and true. But history has shown that his deeds and decisions were evil and oppressive. We have to learn to stop sidling up to power, to detox from the addiction to power and might. It's the way Jesus has shown us from the beginning.

Re-membering is seeing what might not be visible to the eye. Communities that have been erased. Stories that are not told. People who are silenced.

●　●　●　●　●

From 1978 to 2001, at least sixty-five women disappeared from Vancouver's Downtown Eastside, and in 2007 a pig farmer from Port Coquitlam was sentenced to life imprisonment for murdering them. In Canada, the Royal Canadian Mounted Police acknowledged in a 2014 report that more than twelve hundred Indigenous women had gone missing or were murdered between 1980 and 2012.[5] Indigenous women's groups say the number is likely more than four thousand. Indigenous women fifteen years and older are three and a half times more likely to experience violence than non-Indigenous women.

A human rights crisis has been playing itself out—not just in my backyard but across Canada.

In June 2019, the National Inquiry into Missing and Murdered Indigenous Women and Girls published a comprehensive report, saying, "Persistent and deliberate human and Indigenous rights violations and abuses are the root cause behind Canada's staggering rates of violence against Indigenous women, girls, and 2SLGBTQQIA people." During the inquiry, nearly 1,500 testimonies were shared by survivors and family members, fifteen community hearings were held, and more than twenty-three hundred people participated in the truth-gathering process. "This violence amounts to a race-based genocide of Indigenous Peoples, including First Nations, Inuit, and Métis, which especially targets women, girls, and 2SLGBTQQIA people."[6]

The report adds, "This genocide has been empowered by colonial structures, evidenced notably by the *Indian Act*, the Sixties Scoop, residential schools, and breaches of human and Inuit, Métis and First Nations rights, leading directly to the current increased rates of violence, death, and suicide in Indigenous populations."[7] Racism is still killing people.

One of the names of God is El Roi—the God Who Sees (Gen. 16:13–14). God has shown Godself as the One who *sees* those who are hurting, excluded, and missing. But we have not always followed God's lead.

In the parable of the lost sheep, the good shepherd did not rest until the one missing sheep had been found. It did not matter that ninety-nine sheep were safely in the fold; that one sheep mattered (Matt. 18:12–14; Luke 15:3–7). Missing women and girls in our world matter. But I have to keep asking myself, "Do they matter to me? Does my life show that missing women matter?"

Historians estimate that over ten million Indigenous people were living in the Americas when European settlers arrived. By 1900, only about three hundred thousand Indigenous people remained.[8] Millions of people are missing from this continent where I now live.

Why do people go missing? Why are Indigenous women and girls going missing? We have to speak out against the systems that make it possible for them to go missing in the first place. A part of us will always be missing until there is justice, visibility, and acknowledgment of those who are missing. A part of our voices cannot rise until their voices rise.

So let's go looking for the ones who are missing. Let's ask where communities have disappeared to. Let's ask, "Who lived here before? Has this always been here?" When we look for the ones who are missing, we are also re-membering ourselves. When they are lost, erased, or forgotten, we lose, erase, and forget pieces of our own humanity.

When we remember those whom history and racism have tried to erase, we are also re-membered. Together, we are being made whole.

Station of Re-membering

We come to the station of re-membering in the spirit of humility and honor. We come to remember those colonialism, racism and violence have tried to erase or dis-member and we come to be re-membered together.

When my dad passed away in 2021, my dear friends Annie and Kelley sent me a care package from a nonprofit organization called Zatoun. The organization, located in Canada, sells Palestinian products to "create awareness for a just peace for Palestine-Israel."[9] The box had bottles of fair-trade olive oil, dates, herb mix, soap, and coasters—all from Palestine. That olive oil has a special place in our kitchen, and every time I use it, I feel connected to a beautiful global web of love—Kelley, Annie, my dad, and the people of Palestine. Pouring the olive oil becomes re-membering and an embodied prayer for peace.

The care package also included a certificate that three olive trees were planted in Palestine in my dad's memory through an organization called Trees for Life Palestine.[10] In remembering my dad in this way, my family is being re-membered, written into a larger story for justice and peace. In a similar way, I love wearing my bold earrings from local Indigenous designers. Every time I put on these earrings, I celebrate Indigenous creativity, pride, and joy.

What is the invitation for you at the station of re-membering?

▷ REFLECT

- Who or what do you need to re-member?
- Who or what has gone unnoticed by you?
- Which communities have you been warned to stay away from? Why?
- Where have communities been forcibly removed in your nation? How can you re-member that history?
- What is one tangible way you can re-member a group of people that history has tried to dis-member?

The journey of the recovering racist is a journey of re-membering.

18

PRACTICING RESTITUTION

Two hundred fifty years of slavery. Ninety years of Jim Crow. Sixty years of separate but equal. Thirty-five years of racist housing policy. Until we reckon with our compounding moral debts, America will never be whole.

—Ta-Nehisi Coates[1]

Perhaps the only other "r-word" more controversial to American Christians than racism is reparations.

—Jemar Tisby[2]

Two boys—Ahmed and Michael—lived across the street from each other. They grew up together, played together, and rode their bikes together. But one day Michael stole Ahmed's bike. Ahmed confronted Michael, but he didn't get his bike back. The two boys stopped being friends for a while, but Michael really missed his friend, so one day he walked over and asked, "Can we be friends again?" Michael also apologized, and the boys shook hands.

At a party a few days later, Michael told everyone about the bicycle he'd stolen from Ahmed, and Ahmed told everyone how it had made him feel. But then a few months later, Ahmed asked, "Hey, Michael, I know we're friends again. But when are you going to give back my bicycle?"

Michael responded, "Ahmed, this isn't about a bicycle. This is about us becoming friends again. Don't make this about bicycles. I apologized, didn't I?"[3]

This is a simple story meant to begin a complex conversation about restitution. There are several components to restitution, including national, institutional, communal, and personal responsibility.[4] My intention here is for each of us to consider our personal responsibility in the work of restitution.

How do we make right what has been made wrong? How do we address the impact that racism and injustice have had across generations? We need to ask, "Where does my personal story concretely intersect with the larger story of injustice, privilege, and racism?" In South Africa, the conversation has revolved around the word *restitution*; in both Canada and the United States, I've noticed the word *reparations*. I am using the words interchangeably to refer to the idea of making the world more right, including the transfer of wealth and social capital. Ultimately, restitution is about changing the structures that sustain injustice and seeking justice instead.

"Many beneficiaries of apartheid expect those who were oppressed under the old order to just move on as if the past had not happened," says Michael Lapsley, the Anglican priest and social justice activist who lost both hands, an eye, and both eardrums in the anti-apartheid struggle. "Forgiveness and healing relationships involve making restitution for what has been stolen and returning the bike."[5]

● ● ● ● ●

Whiteness has stolen a lot of bikes. And not only bikes—land, language, cultural ceremonies, ideas, wealth, resources, education, even the actual years of people's lives. Recent studies have shown that racism negatively affects the life expectancy of a Black person in the United States.[6]

When we look at injustice, we can easily be overwhelmed by the size of the task. But Ruth Messinger, former president of American Jewish World Service, reminds us, "We cannot retreat to the convenience of being overwhelmed."[7] Although restitution can take on many forms, we always start by listening. Over time, we need to "name the bike" as it applies to our own stories. I have not stolen someone's actual bicycle, but I have benefited from systemic racism. Making restitution requires me to ask, "How specifically did I benefit?" And then, "How may I restore persons affected by that benefit?"

"Take responsibility for benefiting from historical injustice in both material and symbolic ways," suggests Marlyn Faure of the University of Cape Town.[8]

"Have you calculated how much it cost a Black South African person to get you where you are?" René asked me one day during one of our chats. "Have you calculated the cost, my friend?"

Restitution can seem esoteric, but only through the lenses of white privilege. We can make it concrete by breaking down benefit into actual numbers. For example, in 1982 the apartheid government of South Africa spent an average of R1,211 on education for each white child (approximately $65.24 [USD]) and only R146 for each Black child (approximately $7.87). That means every year I received $57.37 more than a Black student toward my education. Over twelve years, that is $688.44 in white privilege. That is racism in actual numbers. And that's only scratching the surface of how I benefited.

Black, Indigenous, and People of Color were often forcibly removed from their homes to create white neighborhoods. Many lost equity in their homes and easy access to their jobs in the cities. Many had to spend more time traveling to and from work. The Bantu Education Act, the law regulating Black education, was intentionally designed to limit Black people's schooling, preparing Black people with skills only to work in manual labor under white control. Black people were not allowed to live in white areas and could not own land in those areas. Black people who stayed in townships also could not own their land. Instead, the apartheid government said Black people should settle in so-called homelands, where they could own land and have political freedom. It was the government's way of keeping the best land for white people. It's difficult to calculate the compounding loss Black, Indigenous, and People of Color have suffered over generations. Still, an actual number, indicating the privilege I received merely for being white when I enrolled in school in South Africa, is one place to start.

• • • • •

When Scott and I began talking about income from this book and how I couldn't write about apartheid or racism and make money from it, the idea was at first a bit hard for him to understand. He was still thinking about the effects of racism in terms of ideology, not relationship.

One day I said to him, "I cannot look my friend René in the eye knowing what I know about her story—how apartheid robbed her family—and take from her again." I wanted to live a different story.

Scott loves René. She has stayed with our family, sat around campfires with us, shared meals and laughter. When I connected my feelings to a person we love and know, he understood. It was a no-brainer. But he wasn't the only one who struggled with the money aspect of restitution. I had been speaking up against racism for years before I was ready to face the fact that racism is not just an idea. It has actual, compounding costs for Black, Indigenous, and People of Color. If I were truly to become serious about anti-racism, I had to get serious about reparations. I had to get serious about money.

When I noticed my resistance, I paid attention. I began asking, "Why? Where does this resistance come from? What is it rooted in?" I interrogated the fears and my ego. Was I willing to humble myself and relinquish power and, in this case, money?

I didn't know how I could be a part of restitution. But I allowed the seed of the idea to grow in my consciousness. I knew that if restitution was seeking justice, I wanted to be a part of it. "Reparations—by which I mean the full acceptance of our collective biography and its consequences—is the price we must pay to see ourselves squarely," says Ta-Nehisi Coates. "What I'm talking about is more than recompense for past injustices—more than a handout, a payoff, hush money, or a reluctant bribe. What I'm talking about is a national reckoning that would lead to spiritual renewal."[9]

* * * * *

In *Another Country: Everyday Social Restitution*, researcher Sharlene Swartz gives this definition of restitution: "Historically and legally, the word 'restitution' has been defined as restoring matters to the state they were before an injustice occurred." She adds, "This is difficult, even impossible to achieve. If, however, we take the word restitution to simply mean, pending a more thorough discussion, 'making things right' for wrongs previously committed, then restitution has numerous possibilities."[10]

It often feels like white people of faith want to wash our hands of the sins of racism, refusing to take responsibility for our part. But recovering from our racism requires a sober moral inventory and then doing our best to make amends—not out of guilt but as part of liberation. Restitution is the right thing to do. We will not be able to move forward until we walk through this door. Jewish biblical scholar Amy-Jill Levine writes in *Light of the World: A Beginner's Guide to Advent*, "'Righteousness' for Luke does not mean having the correct theology. Righteousness means behaving in a way marked by justice."[11] How do people who have been privileged by whiteness now live and behave in a way marked by justice?

The story of the rich young ruler (Mark 10:17–27) reminds us how hard this is for many—the resistance is real. But Zacchaeus offers us another way forward. We meet Zacchaeus, the chief tax collector, in Luke 19. We learn that Zacchaeus is a wealthy man; he also happens to be quite short. When Jesus comes to Zacchaeus's town, Zacchaeus climbs into a sycamore-fig tree to catch a glimpse of this Jesus everyone is talking about. Jesus then invites himself to Zacchaeus's home, and people mutter, "He has gone to be the guest of a sinner." I can certainly relate to Zacchaeus.

Zacchaeus has not been on the side of justice, and yet Jesus invites himself over for a meal. Jesus's generosity also opens Zacchaeus's heart. In fact, he stands up and declares to Jesus, "Look, Lord! Here and now I give half of my possessions to the poor, and if I have cheated anybody out of anything, I will pay back four times the amount" (Luke 19:8). Zacchaeus becomes a leader—an example to us—of restitution. And Jesus responds, "Today salvation has come to this house, because this man, too, is a son of Abraham. For the Son of Man came to seek and to save the lost" (19:9–10). This was not an eschatological statement as much as a declaration of liberation. Levine writes, "For the Jewish Scriptures and for Jews in antiquity, salvation is less an eschatological matter of getting into heaven or having eternal life; nor is it a matter of forgiveness of sin, since they knew that God always forgave the repentant sinner. Salvation means freedom or release from current circumstances: slavery, poverty, ill health, hunger, and thirst."[12]

Salvation is liberation from our chains, which include, I dare say, our ideological chains. For those of us with racist identities—being named racist, oppressor, colonizer—it means

salvation is coming for us too. By doing this work, salvation—
beautiful liberation—will also come to our house.

We can never truly return what whiteness and colonialism
have taken from Black, Indigenous, and People of Color. The
South African finance minister, during a press conference on
reparations for victims following the Truth and Reconciliation
Commission, said, "Even if we take everything Whites have, it
will never make up for what they did."[13]

Lapsley says, "Taking responsibility is the first step in healing, but if we want full reconciliation we have to make material
restitution in the instances where that is possible."[14] We need to
earn trust. We can't just apologize. We have to prove—with our
actions, over time, slowly, humbly, in relationship—that we can
be trusted. "It was not easy for people to believe in an apology
until people saw what perpetrators did with the rest of their lives,
including their money, their time and their energy," says Lapsley.[15]

What am I doing with my money, time, and energy? How
am I working to return the bicycle?

In reflecting on forgiving his perpetrator, Lapsley imagines
having the following conversation: "You know, even though I've
forgiven you, I still have no hands; I still have only one eye; and
I still hear very poorly. Of course, there is nothing you can do
to bring these things back, but because of what you did I will
need assistance for the rest of my life. Of course, you will help
to pay for that." He adds, "Restitution is necessary to fully heal
the relationship between the two of us."[16]

Instead of demanding forgiveness, those of us who have been
privileged need to make efforts to set things right.

Christ calls us to be ministers of reconciliation. Over the
years, I have seen a lot of generosity from Black, Indigenous,
and People of Color around reconciliation, but too often those
of us who are white want to shake the dust off our feet, move
on, and get to reconciliation. We forget the history between
us—paths strewn with shards of glass, broken trust, pain, and

many missing bicycles. We conveniently forget and dismiss the work necessary to repair and heal relationship.

Repair and restitution are not often at the center of conversations. I've learned of a few examples from friends in South Africa. One young family gave their housekeeper the bulk of their income for two months. An Afrikaner woman not only pays the school fees for her housekeeper's daughter but also bought her housekeeper her own home. Several friends give to a monthly education fund for Black students. Other practical acts of restitution can include learning a new language, tutoring students, or financing a small business.

A new story is being written, but not always in the mainstream. We each need to decide in our hearts how we can be a part of restitution.

"When it comes to restitution, there is something for everyone to do: individuals and communities, governments and institutions," adds Swartz. "In order that we do not merely repeat the past, with one group dominating the other, the best way to decide on what actions should be taken is to decide together, in dialogue, with people different to us."[17]

⬤ ⬤ ⬤ ⬤ ⬤

I believe we stand at a threshold—an invitation to a new world beyond whiteness. This new world will require relinquishing the rights and privileges of whiteness. It will require complex thinking and a deep commitment to seeking justice. We have to want righteousness to rise with healing in its wings for collective humanity more than we want our individual flourishing. I also know we won't get to true flourishing unless we embrace restitution and repair.

Can we imagine a world *after* we've made right the wrongs of the past? What could that look like? Perhaps, if we catch a glimpse of that other world that is possible, we will keep doing the work that is required now.

There is no true flourishing of the individual separate from the flourishing of the collective. We have received an invitation to move from defensiveness, denial, numbness, silence, and trauma to being healed and healing, restored and restoring. What do we need to make right?

Jesus is seeking and longing to save us from whiteness now, from the arrogance of white supremacy and from the violence we have perpetrated and keep perpetrating. If you, like me, long not only to become personally whole but also to be a part of making our world more whole, join me in doing the work. Let us reckon with the moral debt of racism. Restitution, too, is liberation.

Station of Restitution

How do you come to the station of restitution today? Come as honestly as you can. What feelings rise in you? What do you sense? How is your body responding? Here is where we come face-to-face with tangible ways to address the injustices of the past. Walking the path of the recovering racist is an invitation to become part of restitution. It's also an invitation to wholeness, liberation, and justice.

Take some time to research organizations and efforts that concentrate on restitution and reparations. Pay attention to stories of restitution that come across your path. How can you join these efforts?

▷ **REFLECT**

- Where do you find yourself in the story of Zacchaeus? What is this story asking you to do?
- How have you uniquely benefited from structural and systemic racism? Can you put a dollar value on the

privilege you have received? If you don't know yet, are you open to leaning in and paying attention to where knowledge may open up to you in the future?

- What stories of restitution and repair are inspiring you?
- Where can you start offering restitution today?

The journey of the recovering racist is a journey that requires restitution.

19

USING POWER FOR GOOD

When the voice of the historically disenfranchised is privileged, what happens to the voice of those who are used to being heard? How will those communities process their discomfort of no longer being the sole voice?

—Mary Dana Hinton[1]

In 2012 I was invited to a table with eleven other women for a Women's Theological Intensive in Bujumbura, Burundi. During the first session together, René handed each of us a sticky note, asking, "What fears do you bring to the table?"

My fear was that I didn't know what to do with my power. I was so mindful of how abusive power had harmed others, including the majority of the women at that table. How do I show up when I have strengths, abilities, and gifts? What do I do with them? Do I rein them in? I wrestled in my soul, not knowing if I should speak these fears out loud. I was one of two white women at the table. I didn't want to turn the attention to me. But we were all asked to share. When my turn came, I shared how I was wrestling with using power for good. I didn't know how to show up.

Joy, a theologian from Kenya, looked at me from across the table and said, "Idelette, we need your voice. You are welcome here. We need you at the table." Joy's words blessed me that day; I still feel her love and her words as a grounding force in my body. But not everybody has a Joy. Not everybody gets to have a Joy speak to our white fears.

I've been affirmed and blessed by many Black people along my journey. That said, Black, Indigenous, and People of Color are not responsible for my liberation. I need to walk this path without seeking their approval or affirmation.

While each of our stories will take its own twists and turns, we need to be mindful of relationship, power dynamics in our relationships, and how these power dynamics play out consistently.

How much space do I take up in the room?

How much space do I take up in the relationship?

Do I speak more than I listen? Or have I learned to listen?

Coming to grips with our power can feel disorienting. Whiteness has made us so used to dominance that holding back can feel like you have not contributed your whole self or "made the best" of a situation. And that is just fine. That is dismantling old ways of being in the world.

I am consistently challenged by Jesus's example of how he used power. As the Son of God and the visible image of the Creator, Jesus did not display all his power all the time. He held back. Even though Jesus had the power to heal all the sick in all of Israel, he didn't. He healed some. Even though he had the power to resist the Roman soldiers, he let them take him, even to his death on the cross.

Just because I can say something does not mean it is my place or time to say it. Then, at other times, I do need to speak up. We need to learn discernment. Power can be used for good. But there are times when white people need to hold back, step back, or even step out.

191

During a weeklong conversation on Robben Island in January 2016, it became clear one day that something in the room needed to shift. All week we'd been participating in a discussion about Jesus and justice. That morning, we'd had a good discussion, and ideas had been captured on big posters all around the room. Then, as we were about to break for tea, facilitators asked for volunteers to help organize the ideas on the giant posters, hoping to save some time.

I stepped up, along with several other people. As I looked around, I noticed that the only people who had stepped up to help organize the ideas were white. I stepped back—concerned, out of sorts, and not sure what to do. But Lisa Sharon Harper, founder and president of Freedom Road, knew exactly what to do. She stepped up to the facilitators and pointed out what was happening in the room. It had been an exercise in power and privilege. She named it.

After the tea break, as all the attendees processed together what had happened, Black, Indigenous, and People of Color spoke up. They needed time to process away from white people. Understandably, some didn't feel free to speak up with white people in the room. There were too many layers of power at work right there.

I was sitting next to a pastor from one of the townships in Cape Town. He hadn't said much the whole time we'd been together, and when he talked to me, I sensed that unspoken power dynamic. All his life he'd been taught to defer to white people. I hated that power dynamic. And I loved him as my fellow human being and co-laborer for justice. I understood that the best thing was for white people to leave the room.

The white people bumbled out of the meeting room a bit disoriented, not quite sure what to do. The door was closed, and most of us went to hang out in the cafeteria area.

Every person there was involved in justice work internationally. We'd never been asked to leave a room. And it was the best thing that could have happened. It was done in love. It was done for a larger cause. It wasn't about white comfort. It was done to set things right at the large and beautiful table of humanity.

When we were called back into the room, there was a tangible shift in power. We sat in a circle together and talked. The conversation dropped to an even deeper, more honest level because this time people who hadn't spoken up all week stood up to share their thoughts. We watched as years of inequality got an adjustment. It was like a chiropractor had come in and realigned power in our body of togetherness. Those who had often stepped back now began to speak up. And those who were comfortable in positions of power, often speaking up, learned to step back.

As white people, sometimes we need to leave the room. We need to get comfortable not holding the mic, not directing the conversation, not volunteering, not taking charge. We need to be mindful of who is at the table, who is speaking, and who stays quiet. In *My Life on the Road*, Gloria Steinem shares this wisdom: "One of the simplest paths to deep change is for the less powerful to speak as much as they listen, and for the more powerful to listen as much as they speak."[2] When you are the person with the most power in the room, listen more and speak less. When you are the person with less power in the room, speak more and listen less.

Power, in itself, is not a bad thing. We want to be empowered, and we want people to have power. But, as people in recovery from our internalized racism, we do need to examine how we use our power.

Power is simply our ability to have an effect.[3] It is our ability to cause change, prevent change, or have influence. Too often power is used to exploit, manipulate, or compete. But power can also be used to meet the needs of others, shift the dynamics in a room, stand up against racism, and build a better life for everyone.

Martin Luther King Jr. said:

Power, properly understood, is the ability to achieve purpose. It is the strength required to bring about social, political or economic changes. In this sense power is not only desirable but necessary in order to implement the demands of love and justice. One of the greatest problems of history is that the concepts of love and power are usually contrasted as polar opposites. Love is identified with a resignation of power and power with a denial of love. . . . What is needed is a realization that power without love is reckless and abusive and that love without power is sentimental and anemic. Power at its best is love implementing the demands of justice. Justice at its best is power correcting everything that stands against love.[4]

As we recover from our racism, we have to learn how to use power for good. Good power doesn't take offense when it is asked to leave the room because it is aligned with love. It is power that does what is necessary for the collective whole. Recovering from our racism is learning to walk in power propelled by love.

● ● ● ● ●

Dr. Chanequa Walker-Barnes, a clinical psychologist, reminds us that whiteness is a dysfunctional system. In addressing the pathology of whiteness, she says, "Culture can be changed and pathology can be healed." We need to name the disease. We also need to actively heal it. There is one thing white people can do, she adds: "Begin to practice little acts of dissent against the pathology of whiteness."[5] Large shifts need to take place to establish justice, but there are small things we can do daily to make the world more right and more just for everyone.

In 2016, while I was on a short trip to South Africa, my mom asked me to go to church with them on Sunday morning. I could see the pleading in her eyes, her longing for me to share her faith, her church, her community. I grew up in the Dutch Reformed Church and had spent the first eighteen years of my life in church every Sunday. Church, in South Africa, came with a lot of baggage for me, not the least of it being the apartheid theology that was created, endorsed, and disseminated by our denomination.

We sat down in church early that morning, and I watched as people trickled in. Rows and rows of perfect pews. There was not one Black, Indigenous, or other Person of Color in that church that morning. More than twenty years after the first democratic election, how could a space in South Africa still be so white? But I was no longer surprised.

Still, my body was on high alert. I was moving through memories of my own past, growing up in this denomination. I was navigating the complexities of love and honor for my parents but fully rejecting that space as a holy communion of saints. When the Communion plate came around, my hand shook as I passed it, refusing to take the bread and the cup. I had been baptized and confirmed in that denomination, but that Sunday I could not take Communion with only white people. I refused. It was such a small act, and yet it was my one small act of dissent.

My mom shuffled uncomfortably next to me. I could feel the anxiety in her body, in my own body, and in the spaces around me. I could feel her displeasure. But I had done the work and could sit in the discomfort. I love my mom so much, *and* I no longer require her approval. I long to look into the face of Jesus and stand with God's heart for justice.

At that time, I didn't know that in 1982 nine Black pastors from South Africa refused to take Communion at a meeting of the leaders of the World Alliance of Reformed Churches in Ottawa, Canada. They refused to take Communion with their white colleagues because they could not yet do it at home in apartheid South Africa.[6] I too had joined in a long prophetic tradition of taking action against an intolerable status quo. So much had changed, and yet so little had changed after apart-heid. While political transformation had come, there had been no transformation in the hearts of most white people. I refuse to participate in Communion in white spaces until transforma-tion comes.

I am reminded of the words of Clarissa Pinkola Estés in an essay to young activists:

> Ours is not the task of fixing the entire world all at once, but of stretching out to mend the part of the world that is within our reach. Any small, calm thing that one soul can do to help an-other soul, to assist some portion of this poor suffering world, will help immensely. It is not given to us to know which acts or by whom, will cause the critical mass to tip toward an endur-ing good.
>
> What is needed for dramatic change is an accumulation of acts, adding, adding to, adding more, continuing. We know that it does not take everyone on Earth to bring justice and peace, but only a small, determined group who will not give up during the first, second, or hundredth gale.[7]

Whether we have much power to change the world or can practice one small act of dissent today, our small acts add up. We can become part of creating a different cultural container.

Beverly Daniel Tatum writes, "The task for Whites is to develop a positive White identity based in reality, not on as-sumed superiority. In order to do that, each person must become aware of his or her Whiteness, recognize that it is personally and socially significant, and learn to feel good about it, not in the sense of a Klan member's 'White pride' but in the context of a commitment to a just society."[8]

White people have been privileged by whiteness for centuries. Privilege can be used to dismantle systems that set up those privileges in the first place. So, while having privilege in itself is not a bad thing, it matters that we own it, name it, see it, and then use it consciously to create a more equal and just world for others. If we have white privilege, we can use that privilege to seek justice and racial equity.

Recovering from our racism is learning to use our power and privilege for good—not just for the good of some but for the good of humanity. For the recovering racists among us, every small step helps us reclaim our humanity.

Station of Power

In Luke 4:18–19 we read how Jesus opened the scroll and echoed the words of the prophet Isaiah:

> The Spirit of the Lord is on me,
>> because he has anointed me
>> to proclaim good news to the poor.
> He has sent me to proclaim freedom for the prisoners
>> and recovery of sight for the blind,
> to set the oppressed free,
>> to proclaim the year of the Lord's favor.

When you read that Scripture passage, where do you find yourself in the story? Sit with that for a moment. Do you see yourself as the person the Spirit of the Lord has anointed?

Is it possible today, as we come with our white lenses, that we are the ones who need recovery of sight now? Or how about needing release from the prison of whiteness? I have often heard this preached and felt a kind of rush to be filled with power so I could be used to help those who are poor, imprisoned, or oppressed. How does it feel to read this passage now from a different place of power?

Then, if Jesus proclaims freedom for prisoners, what does Jesus have to say to those who have created the prisons? What does the Spirit of liberation have to say to our oppressor identity?

Deep breath.

The path of recovering from our racism requires that we learn a new relationship with power. May the Spirit of liberation keep opening our eyes to see and learn new ways of being human in the world.

▷ REFLECT

- What is your relationship with power?
- Which of your identities are dominant in the world—for example, racial, socioeconomic, cultural, gender, sexual, or educational identity? Any of these dominant identities are your privileged identities.
- How can you use your privileged identities for good?

The journey of the recovering racist is a journey of using power for good.

20

RECLAIMING
OUR HUMANITY

"Well, Sojourner, did you always go by this name?"

No, 'deed! My name was Isabella; but when I left the house
of bondage, I left everything behind. I wa'n't goin' to keep
nothin' of Egypt on me, an' so I went to the Lord an' asked
Him to give me a new name. And the Lord gave me Sojourner, because I was to travel up an' down the land,
showin' the people their sins, an' bein' a sign unto them.
Afterwards I told the Lord I wanted another name, 'cause
everybody else had two names; and the Lord gave me Truth,
because I was to declare the truth to the people.

—Sojourner Truth[1]

The word "human" comes from the Latin *humus*, which
means earth. Being human means acknowledging that we're
made from the earth and will return to the earth. We are
earth that has come to consciousness. For a few years we
dance around on the stage of life and have the chance to
reflect a little bit of God's glory. As a human, I'm just a tiny

moment of consciousness, a tiny part of creation, a par-
ticle that reflects only a fragment of God's love and beauty.
And yet that's enough. And then we return to where we
started—in the heart of God. Everything in between is a
school of love.

—Richard Rohr[2]

For centuries, white people made white skin and white ideas
the standard for being human. Feel the violence in those words.

Now imagine the violence of that full sentiment as it ripped
forth into the world, from the first racist pen of Gomes Eanes de
Zurara in the 1400s right through to today.[3] Not as just an idea
but as an idea that pierced, chained, maimed, raped, enslaved,
separated, and killed people.

The creation of this hierarchical world, based on the color of
skin, was and is a violence and a desecration of the *imago Dei*,
the very image of God in every person.[4] Whiteness dehuman-
izes. As white people have perpetuated this false white standard
of being human to the world, it has not only harmed human
beings of Color but also harmed white people, stripping us of
the very thing we said we were.

Give, and you will receive. This equation works not only for
good things but also for the evil we spread into the world. We
give dehumanization, we receive dehumanization.

In *Up from Slavery*, Booker T. Washington shares a conversation he once had with the Honorable Frederick Douglass:

At one time Mr. Douglass was travelling in the state of Pennsylvania, and was forced, on account of his colour, to ride in the
baggage-car, in spite of the fact that he had paid the same price
for his passage that the other passengers had paid. When some
of the white passengers went into the baggage-car to console
Mr. Douglass, and one of them said to him: "I am sorry, Mr.
Douglass, that you have been degraded in this manner," Mr.

Douglass straightened himself up on the box upon which he was sitting, and replied: "They cannot degrade Frederick Douglass. The soul that is within me no man can degrade. I am not the one that is being degraded on account of this treatment, but those who are inflicting it upon me."[5]

The ones who had inflicted the degradation had degraded themselves. So now, those of us who created the so-called standard for being human have to find our way back to our humanity. This is our task as we walk through the valley of the recovering racists. We created and sustained a false image of what it means to be human: a pyramid of whiteness. We bowed and worshiped at its altar. We even made Jesus conform to that white image, giving him blue eyes and light-brown hair. We have desecrated the image of God in our human family for too long.

Our humanity is who we are as human beings. Whiteness says being human looks like this: striving; winning at all costs; imposing yourself on others and on a land, even if you are not welcomed; greed; jealousy; scarcity; superiority; and an arbitrary hierarchy of human worth. Whiteness values wealth more than people. Achievement more than wholeness. Tasks more than relationships. Being right more than being kind. But this is not the humanity I want to belong to or be a part of creating.

Resmaa Menakem reminds us that "we will not end white-body-supremacy—or any form of human evil—by trying to tear it to pieces. Instead, we can offer people better ways to belong, and better things to belong to. Instead of belonging to a race, we can belong to a culture. Each of us can also build our own capacity for genuine belonging."[6] So, either we are sustaining that old paradigm—and lie—of what it means to be human, or we are part of aligning ourselves with the full and glorious image of humanity that has always been true. Every person is created in the image of God.

How do we go about reclaiming our humanity? We can't do it by skipping ahead and running to the beautiful hope of unity and belonging. We can't skip to kumbaya without wrestling with the centuries of dehumanization we have been a part of.

● ● ● ● ●

In Genesis we read the story of Jacob and Esau, twin sons born to Isaac and Rebekah. Esau is the eldest son, and in chapter 25 we learn that Jacob tricks him into handing over his birthright for a bowl of red lentil stew. But this is not where Jacob's treachery stops. When Esau is forty years old, Isaac is old and weak and can no longer see well. He calls Esau into his tent, wanting to impart his final blessing. But first he asks Esau to go out and hunt some wild game and prepare him the tasty food he loves to eat. Rebekah hears her husband's instructions to their eldest son, and while Esau is out hunting, she conspires with Jacob and prepares a meal of goat's meat. Before Esau returns, Jacob goes into his father's tent and tricks their dad into giving him the blessing instead.

Jacob takes what isn't his. Esau loses everything and hates Jacob for it. After fleeing, Jacob begins working for his uncle Laban and makes a new life in Paddan Aram. In exchange for seven years of work, Laban promises his daughter Rachel to Jacob as a wife. But when the time comes, Laban tricks Jacob into marrying Leah, his eldest daughter, instead. Jacob is reaping what he has sown, and he has to work another seven years before he can marry Rachel.

Jacob, someone who has stolen from his brother, asks to prove his honesty to his father-in-law. In fact, he says, "My honesty will testify for me." I wonder if Jacob has to prove to himself, too, that he can be trusted. Not only does he deceive his brother and his own father, but he acts against his own integrity. By robbing others, he robs himself. Slowly, year after year, a new character has to be formed. He has to reclaim his humanity.

After twenty years of serving Laban and looking after his flocks, Jacob is called by God back to the land of his father. On their journey home, Jacob and his household set up camp at Mahanaim. Jacob knows there will come a reckoning—he will have to face Esau. So he sends messengers ahead of them to prepare the way for their meeting. When the messengers come back, they say that Esau is on his way and has four hundred men with him. Jacob is shaking in his leather sandals. After dividing the people with him into two groups—so in case Esau attacks one group, the other can escape—Jacob turns to God in prayer.

After praying, he prepares a huge gift for his brother. I wonder if God had softened Jacob's heart toward restitution. He can never make up for what he stole, but he can begin to set things right. He sends a whole barnyard full of animals ahead of him as gifts to Esau. While the gifts go ahead, Jacob stays in the camp. There is more work for him to do.

That night, Jacob wrestles with a man the text says is God. Jacob's hip is wrenched as he wrestles with the man. They wrestle until daybreak, and still Jacob will not let go. What needs to be shaped in Jacob through this wrestling?

"I will not let you go until you bless me," Jacob says.

He has learned that stealing someone else's blessing does not actually bless. The man who stole his brother's birthright and his blessing is still desperate for a blessing. What he doesn't know is that he also needs a new name. Jacob receives the name Israel. He had struggled with God and humans and had overcome. He receives not only the blessing he had longed for but also a new name. It is another step in reclaiming his humanity.

We are Jacob. We have stolen the birthright and blessing of Black, Indigenous, and People of Color. We were meant to be family—to walk together as human siblings. But we decided to deceive and trick and steal our siblings' blessing. Now, we don't just dare walk up to Esau and pretend like nothing happened. Before we can meet our brothers and sisters to make things right and be reconciled, we have to wrestle. We have to wrestle with what we have done, and we have to wrestle with who we have become.

We, as white people, have to wrestle with God, the Spirit of liberation, and the history we have written on this earth until we may also find our own liberation. We have to face the shadow side of white consciousness and make restitution—send a whole barnyard ahead—as we prepare to meet up with our siblings. If we want to reclaim our humanity, we can't just do it individually by facing our personal shadow self. We have to face the shadow self in our collective consciousness. We have to take responsibility for the history our ancestors wrote on the earth.

Stand in the Cape Coast Castle in Ghana as enslaved people are sold off.

We are the slave traders.

Stand on the deck of the slave ship *Zong* as Captain Luke Collingwood orders more than 130 enslaved people to be thrown overboard to drown just so insurance will cover their deaths.[7]

We are Captain Luke Collingwood.

Get into the belly of a ship full of enslaved people and make the voyage across the Atlantic.

We are the owners of those slave ships.

Feel the shackles on the necks, around the ankles, and around the wrists of those on whom we have placed those chains.

We are the owners of enslaved people.

Stand in the gas chambers and be present to the fear and the pain.

We are the ones who turned on the gas.

Stand in the crowd at a racial terror lynching.

We are the ones who cheered at the suffering and murders of our brothers and sisters.

We are the knee on the neck of Mr. George Floyd.

We are Gomes Eanes de Zurara.

We are H. F. Verwoerd.

We are David Duke.

We are Donald Trump.

Take a deep breath.

Stay here as long as you need to. Come back and keep doing the work. The person we least want to associate with, the person or persons who have been the most vile in this history of whiteness, is where we need to see ourselves.

Pause. Breathe. Place a hand on your heart to remind you that you are so deeply loved.

Where do you need to go and stand? Which part of history do you need to own?

● ● ● ● ●

In the Zulu language, people greet each other with *Sawubona*. It means, "I see you." It recognizes the worth and dignity of each person. By saying "Sawubona," we honor the other person with our words, our presence, and our attention to their humanity. The spirit of Sawubona is beholding each other as equals and living in a way that affirms that.

We are each wrestling for a new name. As white people, we have been called oppressor, enslaver, thief, murderer, colonizer, racist. The story we are writing now and the wrestling we are doing will determine what name you and I will be called by history.

When I began this journey of anti-racism and reclaiming my humanity, I did not feel like I deserved to be part of the larger human story. That was my deepest pain. I imagined God like a mama bear, guarding the door to the circle of humanity. Another voice hissed, "You don't deserve to enter in. You messed up. Your people messed up. Stay out. You don't get to go into the Holy of Holies. Your hands are covered with injustice. Stay out!"

Then in 2008, the preschool class of my daughter Gabi sponsored a little girl from Botshabelo in South Africa. I carried her name with me on my heart and in our prayers around the dinner table for months. She was the first opening to any possibility of relationship across the giant divide apartheid had created. I felt unworthy, so I just prayed for her and her family. I lifted her before the God of the universe like I would one of my own children. We did that for months, and then, as we were planning to go to South Africa, I wondered whether there might be a way to visit her family. I emailed World Vision, and they said not to be too hopeful. But within days the team in Botshabelo had responded with an enthusiastic yes. We immediately reorganized our trip, rented a car, and drove nearly five hundred kilometers from Pretoria to Botshabelo just so we could meet her and her family.

As we drove into Bloemfontein, the city right outside Botshabelo, the hot February air felt thick with frenzy, fear, and pent-up anger. I felt the ripple effects of the injustice of apartheid in the air all around me. It didn't help that an angry white driver swore and waved his fists at us. Even now, as Scott and I talk about that night, we remember the frenetic atmosphere.

I slept very little. I wrestled with God all night.

While I sensed that this had been an invitation, a gate, to enter into the full and beautiful circle of humanity, I did not feel worthy. The history of my people haunted me. We had injustice on our hands. My privilege and education cost others much, including the very people we were going to visit. I had excluded; now I wanted to be included. I had brought my family to eat from the goodness of inclusion. Shame was hissing very loudly, "You have no right here. You don't deserve to be allowed in. How dare you?"

We drove out to Botshabelo early the next morning. My body kept bracing itself, waiting for the gate to slam shut in my face. But it didn't. A minivan waited for us at the entrance into Botshabelo and escorted us all the way to the World Vision compound just so we could easily find it. As we approached, my daughters excitedly pointed to a poster taped to the outside wall, right in front of where we parked. Someone had written in large letters: Welcome Home, McVicker Family.

Welcome *home*.

I felt those words so deeply in my heart. That most generous invitation was more than I, a daughter of apartheid, could have ever hoped for or imagined. As I got out of the car that morning, deep in my soul, I knew a gate had opened up. I was crossing a threshold. I was entering into a new story. I felt tender and grateful, honoring the gift of being welcomed in.

My heart would have crawled in that day. But women and children, teachers and librarians met me there, as equals. I didn't have to crawl. I could walk with such joy. I could look people in the eye. I didn't have to wear my old story like a banner. There was a new banner of belonging written for me: Welcome Home.

At home, we are not meant to crawl. At home, our shoulders can relax, and we can exhale into the comfort of belonging. Here we are already so loved.

We all belong in the circle of humanity. But we don't get to walk in bringing old, domineering, oppressive ways. Before we may enter, we have to show that we are committed to a different world—a world in which love is the essence and justice flows like a river.

God knows and sees our hearts. Are they soft, repentant, humble? Are they willing to receive grace? Are they willing to learn new ways? Are they willing to make peace? Are they hungry for newness and a more beautiful belonging? Author Osheta Moore writes, "The most heartbreaking thing I hear from a White Peacemaker is, 'I'm just White.' No! You're not just White; you were intentionally made to live confidently in your skin by a good God. Every single person on this planet is a reflection of the image of God, *imago Dei*. What's not good is how this culture has codified your expression of the *imago*

Dei and nullified mine. This is our work together . . . : to re-claim humanity for both of us and create a counterculture that actively exposes and resists the violence of white supremacy culture."[8] *Amen.*

Every step we take deeper into our recovery is a becoming. We are on a journey to find better ways to belong and to create a culture of beloved humanity.

Station of Humanity

The station of humanity starts with honoring the humanity of those who have been dehumanized. That is central.

Reflect on the symbol of a triangle. Whiteness has built a hierarchy of worth in the shape of a triangle, much like a pyramid. Hold that in your consciousness. What comes up for you? How has this affected Black, Indigenous, and People of Color? Where are you in the pyramid? What else is coming to mind for you?

Now reflect on the image of a circle. Who belongs in the circle of humanity? What are the values in the circle? Who gets to enter in? How do we enter in? What has whiteness communicated to you about what it means to be human? What does it mean to you to be human now?

Find a way to open up entry to a large circle of humanity. Find a picture, make a drawing, a painting, a song, an embroidery, or a poem—however you would like to express it. Is the gate to a larger circle of humanity open or closed for you? How does that feel? If it is closed, pay attention to how that feels. Entering the large circle of humanity is a holy invitation. Do not rush. Do not employ colonialist methods—busting through gates that have not been open yet or asserting yourself to take something by any or all means. Stay with the discomfort and the exclusion. Pay attention to how that feels. Be mindful of how many were left out of belonging in the pyramid of whiteness.

Pray. Watch and wait patiently, determinedly. This is a holy waiting. I'm so grateful you are here. Thank you for doing the work.

▷ REFLECT

- What has whiteness communicated to you about what it means to be human?
- What has whiteness communicated to you about what it means to belong?
- What does it mean to you to be human now?
- Are there gates of belonging that have remained closed for you? Why do you think is that?
- Write or share a commitment to keep going on this journey of recovering from your racism.

The journey of the recovering racist is a journey of reclaiming our humanity.

AFTERWORD

In the school I attended growing up, we had a Latin motto: *Sol Iustitiae Illustra Nos*, which I was told means "the sun of righteousness shines on us." As I started listening to different stories and wrestling with my place in the story of injustice, I became very angry with that motto. I thought, *What audacity for us as an all-white school at that time to imagine that the sun of righteousness—or justice—was shining on us.* How far we had wandered from God's heart for justice, and yet how emboldened we were by this interpretation of being divinely sanctioned and deserving of God's favor. It was a shining example of our deeply embedded exceptionalism.

I wrestled with those words for years. That school had been such a formative part of my life and is still a part of my community—full of people I love and care about. I didn't know how to hold all of the feelings—love for the people, anger at the exceptionalism and racism, and a burning hope for change. For years, I have longed for transformation not only in my school community but also in the larger Afrikaner community. Then I learned that these words could be translated as more of a request or a prayer: Sun of righteousness, shine on us. I also began hearing the words of the motto alongside the words in

Malachi 4:2. Here the prophet says, "The sun of righteousness shall rise, with healing in its rays." What a statement of promise. Holding the old school motto alongside Malachi's words, a prayer began to form in my heart. Where change had once felt hopeless, I began to feel a sprinkling of hope—a new day could dawn with healing in its wings. We are not there yet, but I am believing. I hold on to the hope that a new world is possible. I hold on to the hope that dry, white bones can live and become anti-racist. I say these words now as a prayer, a hope for what is to come:

> Sun of righteousness,
> May you rise with healing from arrogance.
> Healing from ignorance.
> Healing from naivete.
> Healing from any sense of superiority.
>
> Sun of righteousness,
> May you rise with healing from our racism.
> Healing for those traumatized by racist systems,
>   policies, laws, actions, words, and ideas.
> Healing for the wounds we have inflicted.
> Healing from injustice.
>
> Sun of righteousness,
> May you rise with healing from defensiveness.
> Healing from justification.
> Healing from shame.
> Healing from blame.
>
> Sun of righteousness,
> Rise in us.
> Rise on all of us.
> Rise on beloved humanity.

Oh, how I long for the sun of justice to shine on all of us as humanity. Oh, how I long for healing for our world.

A CONFESSION FOR RECOVERING RACISTS

We acknowledge . . .

We acknowledge the injustice of race and racism and the harm it has inflicted on generations of people across centuries.

We acknowledge that we have benefited from the story of race and racism.

We acknowledge that the Bible has been used to perpetuate racism, both consciously and unconsciously.

We acknowledge that we have participated in and perpetuated—either consciously or unconsciously— the myth of white body supremacy.

We acknowledge that racism has been embedded in our DNA, and we have committed to working toward its dismantling, not only in the world but within our own bodies.

We acknowledge the dignity and inherent worth of every person in this world.

We acknowledge that we do not require forgiveness from those we have oppressed or harmed.

We acknowledge that our freedom and flourishing is connected to the freedom and flourishing of others.

We repent . . .

We repent of the ways we have participated in creating and sustaining hierarchies of worth.

We repent of the ways we have harmed others, whether consciously or unconsciously.

We repent of the systems and structures we have created to benefit only some and oppress others.

We repent of centering white bodies, white voices, and white experiences.

We repent of our entitlement to attention, to the center of the story, to recognition.

We repent of our addiction to being the hero in a story.

We repent of our addiction to dominance and power.

We repent of our addiction to individualism.

We repent of our need for validation.

We repent of our need to be affirmed as a "good person."

We repent of taking what was never ours to take, whether land, place, persons, position, title, or wealth.

We have committed . . .

We have committed to seeking racial justice.

We have committed to taking responsibility for any power and privilege we have and we endeavor to use it not to harm but to seek justice.

We have committed to making a fearless inventory of how we have personally and specifically benefited from systems and structures of racial oppression, and we have committed to doing our best to redress it in our lifetime.

We have committed to being part of repairing our world.

We have committed to learning, unlearning, and recalibrating our minds and our bodies for as long as racial oppression exists in our world.

We have committed to honoring every person on this earth for their inherent worth, including ourselves.

We have committed to understanding our unique cultural heritage and the stories we come from.

We have committed to building our capacity for true and beautiful belonging.

We have committed to listening to the anger of those who have suffered oppression, so we may hear the truth.

We have committed to getting comfortable with discomfort.

We have committed to joining efforts that dismantle systems and structures of oppression.

We have committed to choosing love to implement the demands of justice.

We have committed to the long walk of love and liberation.

We have committed to a life of racial sobriety.

The journey of the recovering racist is a journey of love.

ACKNOWLEDGMENTS

As I write these acknowledgments, I am in the Strand in South Africa, back in the land of my birth and my heart. Through the windows of my mom's apartment, I can see the Helderberg Mountains, and I am mindful of the Indigenous people of South Africa who have been here from the very first sunrise. Most of the history I was told about this land was wrong. I am grateful to activists around the world who tell us the truth and compel me to do better. I sit at your feet.

I wrote most of this book as a guest on the unceded territories of the Kwantlen people, the Semiahmoo people, and the Stó:lō people in the country known as Canada. I am so grateful for the welcome, generosity, and hospitality I have been afforded as an immigrant on this land.

I am grateful to all people across so many generations who have struggled for liberation, love, and dignity both in South Africa and also around the world. I am especially indebted to the work of the archbishop emeritus Desmond Tutu, former president Nelson Mandela, Robert Sobukwe, and professor Jonathan D. Jansen. Your work and your love have liberated so many, including this very grateful Afrikaans woman.

This book has been my effort to capture the ways out of the separateness I once felt so deeply in my soul. Over and over again, love showed me that separateness—that old apartheid—was never the plan. Needless to say, I have done this work in a web of love.

Scott, when I first met you, I immediately felt at home with you. You showed me that I could come home to a person. You have witnessed me wrestling with my past for as long as we have known each other. You have never dismissed my pain. You have listened and you have believed. Thank you, also, for walking with me down the paths of restitution. Thank you for your love.

Gabi, Telah, and Shay, thank you for how you have cheered me on and understood that your mom needs to do this—also for your liberation. Much of this book was written for you. There are parts of me you may never know, because of the language barrier, but I hope you now understand better. My hope is that you can live a different story and be part of a liberating reality in our world.

To my parents, who haven't always known what to do with their creative, feminist, defiant daughter and yet have always loved me. Thank you for understanding that I needed to do this work. Pa, I know now that you cheer me on from the other side. It has strengthened me. Ma, thank you for giving me permission to write the hard things. I honor you.

To Dorothea, who took me under her wing in Taiwan and embodied how Jesus loves and liberates. You have never allowed me to choose shame or smallness; you have always steered me toward love. Thank you for mothering me, like only you can.

To René August, so much of this book is about a liberation you have sparked. I love that we get to journey in this generation together. Your love is expansive and beautiful. I will never forget when you said on Robben Island, "Now pray in the language of your dreams." You have consistently challenged me to go deeper, be more honest, and not settle for anything less than our collective liberation. You are one of the most beautiful human beings I know. I love you.

To Nicole Joshua, whether we are on Zoom together or in Canada, Uganda, Burundi, or South Africa, you are a soul sister. My heart is at home with you. You are very wise, and I learn so much from you. I couldn't have written this book without your love and friendship. I treasure you.

To Kelley Nikondeha, my soul sister, I couldn't have done this without your wisdom in charting a path. I look forward to many more adventures together—literary and otherwise. There is nobody like you.

To Tina Francis-Mutungu, you are family to me. I treasure our long conversations and how we can go deep right away. Thank you for reminding me about "passionate detachment." I want to go everywhere in this world with you.

To Diane, you took a chance on friendship and I am forever grateful.

To the Circle of Awesome—Kathleen, Shaley, and Courtney—I will never forget that first meeting of the recovering racists, sitting on a hill with our lawn chairs six feet apart, navigating both the global pandemic and our place in systemic racism. Then there was the Zoom meeting when you helped me discern whether I should send off the proposal. I couldn't have done it without you. I am so grateful I don't have to journey alone—you have helped to heal so much of the apartheid in me.

To the SheLoves leadership team, over the years and especially now as we have navigated so many cycles of change, longing to seek justice and sisterhood. What a sacred space we are. Thank you for being women who love profoundly.

To the SheLoves community and all those in the Dangerous Women community who consistently remind me that a different world is possible. This kind of expansive, justice-seeking love was once only an idea. You show me, daily, that it is real.

It is such an honor to walk with you and to sit in the circle of global sisterhood with you.

To Leah Kostamo, my spiritual director, who listened to me one day and said, "Well, the book is not being written, but the character is being formed." Thank you for seeing me.

To Sarah Bessey, for always being one of my greatest cheerleaders. You inspire me.

To Jessica Goudeau, Danielle Mayfield, Christiana Peterson, Amy Peterson, and Stina Kielsmeier-Cook for believing in me, even when this book took so much longer than any of yours. I had to write my own way forward and you understood.

To Esmé Bouwer, who once saw and loved a very broken South African girl. Thank you.

To Ellie and Doug—years ago, you invited me to your home where I could spend the whole weekend writing in your basement. You made space for my dreams when I didn't know how to believe in them myself. I am so deeply grateful for your love.

To Anje, Jeanmari, and Herman. I love you.

Thank you to my Canadian family for embracing me and loving me. I love laughing with you. With you, I kick off my shoes.

To my agent Rachelle Gardner, who has believed in me and knew when I was ready but also when I was not. You never rushed this project and for that, I will be eternally grateful. Thank you for being such a beautiful champion for liberating voices.

Thank you to Katelyn Beaty and the team at Brazos Press. You took a chance on me, and I am so grateful.

To Lindiwe, who read the manuscript and gave me the feedback I desperately longed to hear. I am so honored to build a different world with you.

To Leah Abraham. I treasure our Tuesday morning meetings and your honesty, grit, and creativity.

Thank you to Siki. I am so honored to know you, pray with you, and laugh with you. I love you, my sister.

Thank you to Ms. Blom, my high school English teacher. You taught me not only to love the English language but to love what the language could do to connect humanity.

To my godchild, Joh-Mari: I believe in you. May you and your generation write a different story.

To the women of the Black Sash: when I couldn't see my own ancestors as people of the light yet, your work showed me that women could be united across everything that divides us and could march for justice. I needed to know that. Thank you for your work.

To the Afrikaner people, as hard as this may be to swallow, I love you. I believe we can find better ways of belonging.

Thank you to the authors of books on anti-racism, anti-apartheid, and liberation who have been my teachers. I was once lost and desperately hungry in the desert of whiteness. You have awakened me, taught me, fed me, and liberated me. The journey continues. I hope I may say thank you, in some small way, with my life.

To Lisa Sharon Harper, the world does not have enough thank-yous. Thank you, thank you, thank you. Oh, how I wish we could spend another week together on Robben Island.

To God, the Liberator of my soul and the Liberator of all people. You are why I did this. I lifted up my eyes to these same Helderberg Mountains so many decades ago, longing for a different world. I didn't know it was possible then—it was just a hunch—but your Spirit has compelled me to keep believing, keep trusting my intuition, and keep looking for love. I stand in awe.

NOTES

Introduction

1. Ibram X. Kendi, *How to Be an Antiracist* (New York: One World, 2019), 13.

2. Tessa McWatt, *Shame on Me: An Anatomy of Race and Belonging* (Toronto: Random House, 2019), 22.

3. For more about whiteness and white supremacy, see Desmond Cole, *The Skin We're In* (New York: Doubleday, 2020), 7–9.

4. Rachel Ricketts, *Do Better: Spiritual Activism for Fighting and Healing from White Supremacy* (New York: Atria, 2021), xv.

5. Ijeoma Oluo, *So You Want to Talk about Race* (New York: Hachette, 2018), 19.

6. Some resources on white privilege include Layla F. Saad, *Me and White Supremacy* (Naperville, IL: Sourcebooks, 2020), 33–39; Oluo, *So You Want to Talk about Race*, 53–69; and Tiffany Jewell, *This Book Is Anti-Racist* (Minneapolis: Quarto, 2020), 134–37.

7. "Talking about Race: Whiteness," Smithsonian National Museum of African American History and Culture, accessed March 26, 2021, https://nmaahc.si.edu/learn/talking-about-race/topics/whiteness.

8. Willie James Jennings, *After Whiteness: An Education in Belonging* (Grand Rapids: Eerdmans, 2020), 9.

9. Osheta Moore, *Dear White Peacemakers: Dismantling Racism with Grit and Grace* (Harrisonburg, VA: Herald, 2021), 34.

10. Robben Island Museum Publication, "Chapter 3: Cultural Landscapes," accessed March 30, 2021, https://www.robben-island.org.za/files/publications/Integrated%20conservation%20management%20plan/icmp_chapt3.pdf.

11. Pan Africanist Congress of Azania, "Sobukwe is a man with a magnetic personality, great organising ability, and a divine sense of mission," Facebook, December 29, 2020, https://www.facebook.com/PACofUnity/posts/read-in-1964-the-entire-south-african-parliament-met-to-discuss-one-man-mangalis/1187396441719610/.

12. "Ruby Sales: Where Does It Hurt?," *On Being* with Krista Tippett, September 15, 2016, https://onbeing.org/programs/ruby-sales-where-does-it -hurt/.

13. "Robin DiAngelo and Resmaa Menakem: Towards a Framework for Repair," *On Being* with Krista Tippett, July 9, 2020, https://onbeing.org/programs /robin-diangelo-and-resmaa-menakem-towards-a-framework-for-repair/.

14. Read Rachel Ricketts's entire chapter "Impact over Intention," in *Do Better*, 175–84.

15. Cole Arthur Riley (@BlackLiturgies), "Being numb to the knife in your hand doesn't make it any less sharp. . . . God, heal the wounds made in the dark," Instagram, February 7, 2021, www.instagram.com/p/CK_tJaghqAP /?igshid=11hto8d9bocsf.

16. Lisa Sharon Harper, *The Very Good Gospel: How Everything Wrong Can Be Made Right* (Colorado Springs: WaterBrook, 2016), 11–13.

17. The term *good ancestors* is from the work of Layla F. Saad, including her *Good Ancestor Podcast*. For more information about becoming a good ancestor, read her book, Layla F. Saad, *Me and White Supremacy: Combat Racism, Change the World, and Become a Good Ancestor* (Naperville, IL: Sourcebooks, 2020).

18. I use the word *kin-dom* following the example of mujerista theologian Ada María Isasi-Díaz. She writes: "I use the 'kin-dom' of God to avoid using the sexist and elitist word 'kingdom.' Also, the sense of family of God that 'kin-dom' represents is much in line with the centrality of family in our Latina culture. I am grateful to Georgene Wilson, O.S.F., from whom I learned this word." Ada María Isasi-Díaz, *Mujerista Theology: A Theology for the Twenty-First Century* (Maryknoll, NY: Orbis Books, 1996), 83.

19. "This Is Restitution," The Restitution Foundation, accessed March 23, 2021, https://www.restitution.org.za/.

20. Constance Grady, "Why the Term "BIPOC" Is So Complicated, Explained by Linguists," Vox, June 30, 2020, https://www.vox.com/2020/6/30/21300294 /bipoc-what-does-it-mean-critical-race-linguistics-jonathan-rosa-deandra-miles -hercules.

Part 1 Wake Up

1. Andre Henry, "Hope and Hard Pills," email newsletter, February 27, 2021, https://mailchi.mp/hopeandhardpills.com/slogans-13357983.

2. Thomas Norman DeWolf and Jodie Geddes, *The Little Book of Racial Healing* (New York: Good Books, 2019), 91.

3. Richard Rohr, *Falling Upward: A Spirituality for the Two Halves of Life* (San Francisco: Jossey-Bass, 2011), x.

Chapter 1 Acknowledging Our Racism

1. Emmanuel Acho, "Uncomfortable Conversations with a Black Man," YouTube, June 3, 2020, https://youtu.be/h8jUA7JBkF4.

2. Austin Channing Brown, *I'm Still Here: Black Dignity in a World Made for Whiteness* (New York: Convergent, 2018), loc. 408 of 652, Kindle.

3. Quoted by Melinda D. Anderson (@mdawriter), "The person who calls himself 'The least racist person in the room' is always the most racist. African American proverb," Twitter, October 22, 2020, 8:26 p.m., https://twitter.com/mdawriter/status/1319463322757070850.

4. John Dugard, "Convention on the Suppression and Punishment of the Crime of Apartheid," Audiovisual Library of International Law, November 30, 1973, https://legal.un.org/avl/ha/cspca/cspca.html.

5. I am deeply indebted to the collective work of Ibram X. Kendi, including *Be Anti-Racist: A Journal for Awareness, Reflection, and Action* (New York: One World, 2020).

6. John 8:32: "Then you will know the truth, and the truth will set you free."

7. The term *white fragility* was coined by Robin DiAngelo. For more on this idea, read Robin DiAngelo, *White Fragility: Why It's So Hard for White People to Talk About Racism* (Boston: Beacon, 2018).

8. Hein Willemse, "More Than an Oppressor's Language: Reclaiming the Hidden History of Afrikaans," The Conversation, April 27, 2017, https://theconversation.com/more-than-an-oppressors-language-reclaiming-the-hidden-history-of-afrikaans-71838.

9. Vivian Chou, "How Science and Genetics Are Reshaping the Race Debate of the 21st Century," Harvard University: The Graduate School of Arts and Sciences, April 17, 2017, https://sitn.hms.harvard.edu/flash/2017/science-genetics-reshaping-race-debate-21st-century.

10. Nell Irvin Painter, *The History of White People* (New York: Norton, 2010), 391.

11. Natalie Angier, "Do Races Differ? Not Really, Genes Show," *New York Times*, August 22, 2000, https://www.nytimes.com/2000/08/22/science/do-races-differ-not-really-genes-show.html.

12. Ta-Nehisi Coates, *Between the World and Me* (New York: Spiegel & Grau, 2015), 7.

13. Isabel Wilkerson, *Caste: The Origins of Our Discontents* (New York: Random House, 2020), 17.

14. Ibram X. Kendi, *How to Be an Antiracist* (New York: One World, 2019), 221.

15. Resmaa Menakem, *My Grandmother's Hands: Racialized Trauma and the Pathway to Mending Our Hearts and Bodies* (Las Vegas: Central Recovery, 2017), 14.

16. Bessel van der Kolk, *The Body Keeps the Score: Brain, Mind and Body in the Healing of Trauma* (New York: Viking, 2014), 1.

17. Arica L. Coleman, "James Baldwin Documentary 'I Am Not Your Negro' Is the Product of a Specific Moment in History," Time.com, February 24, 2017, https://time.com/4680673/james-baldwin-documentary-history/.

18. Wilkerson, *Caste*, 17.

19. Marley K., "Yes My Dear, All White People Are Racists," Age of Awareness, June 6, 2020, https://medium.com/age-of-awareness/yes-all-white-people-are-racist-eefa97cc5605.

20. *Macmillan Dictionary*, s.v. "acknowledge," accessed May 15, 2021, https://www.macmillandictionary.com/us/dictionary/american/acknowledge.

Chapter 2 Awakening

1. Anthony de Mello, *The Way to Love* (New York: Image Books, 1995), 134.

2. Peter Dickens, "To Fully Reconcile the Boer War Is to Fully Understand the 'Black' Concentration Camps," South African History Online, accessed March 27, 2021, https://www.sahistory.org.za/archive/fully-reconcile-boer-war-fully -understand-black-concentration-camps-peter-dickens.

3. Hermann Giliomee, *Die Afrikaners: 'n Biografie* (Kaapstad: Tafelberg, 2004), 211.

Part 2 Leave

1. I borrow this phrase with deep respect and gratitude from the autobiography of former South African president Nelson Mandela. See Nelson Mandela, *A Long Walk to Freedom* (London: Abacus, 1994).

2. Robin DiAngelo, *White Fragility: Why It's So Hard for White People to Talk about Racism* (Boston: Beacon, 2018).

3. Vean Ima Torto (@vean_ima), Instagram, June 2, 2020, https://www.insta gram.com/p/CA9l0RtgdGm. Used with permission.

4. In *Stamped: Racism, Antiracism, and You*, Jason Reynolds and Ibram X. Kendi name "The World's First Racist" as Gomes Eames de Zurara. Zurara wrote a biography of the life of Prince Henry of Portugal, including the prince's trade in enslaved people. His book was called *The Chronicle of the Discovery and Conquest of Guinea*, and it was the first "recorded history of anti-Black racist ideas" (Reynolds and Kendi, *Stamped: Racism, Antiracism, and You* [New York: Little, Brown and Company, 2020], 7). See also Ibram X. Kendi, *Stamped from the Beginning: The Definitive History of Racist Ideas in America* (New York: Bold Type, 2016), 22–30. For a substantial account of Zurara's ideas, especially while documenting a transaction that occurred in 1444, see Willie James Jennings, *The Christian Imagination: Theology and the Origins of Race* (New Haven: Yale, 2010), 15–20.

Chapter 3 Imagining a Different World

1. Andre Henry, "Hope and Hard Pills," email newsletter, February 27, 2021, https://mailchi.mp/hopeandhardpills.com/slogans-13357983.

2. Anthony Smith, "Prophets are dangerous. But dangerous to the status quo . . . ," Facebook, January 15, 2018, https://www.facebook.com/anthony.smith .372/posts/10156169477907174. Used with permission.

3. Steven Charleston, *Ladder to the Light: An Indigenous Elder's Meditations on Hope and Courage* (Minneapolis: Broadleaf, 2021), 17.

4. Desmond M. Tutu, "Desmond Tutu: A God of Surprises," interview by Krista Tippett, *On Being* with Krista Tippett, April 29, 2010, https://onbeing.org /programs/desmond-tutu-a-god-of-surprises/#transcript.

5. Desmond M. Tutu, *No Future without Forgiveness* (London: Rider, 1999), 3.

6. Isabel Wilkerson, *Caste: The Origins of Our Discontents* (New York: Random House, 2020), 151.

7. Nikita Steward, "'I've Been to the Mountaintop,' Dr. King's Last Sermon Annotated," *New York Times*, April 2, 2018, https://www.nytimes.com/interactive/2018/04/02/us/king-mlk-last-sermon-annotated.html.

Chapter 4 Getting Comfortable with Discomfort

1. "Message from the International Council of 13 Indigenous Grandmothers," Findhorn New Story Hub, May 19, 2019, http://newstoryhub.com/2019/05/message-from-the-international-council-of-13-indigenous-grandmothers.

2. Ta7talíya Nahanee, *Decolonize First: A Liberating Guide and Workbook for Peeling Back the Layers of Neocolonialism* (Squamish, BC: Nahanee Creative, 2020), 12.

3. See their website at www.bpfna.org.

4. Cornel West, "Courage," in *Readings for Diversity and Social Justice*, ed. Maurianne Adams, Warren J. Blumenfeld, R. Castaneda, Heather W. Hackman, Madeline L. Peters, and Ximena Zuniga (New York: Routledge, 2013), 625.

Chapter 5 Facing Ugly Truth

1. Dr. Chanequa Walker-Barnes, "Pathological Whiteness: Diagnosing the Hidden Wound," TheoEd Talks, Vimeo, March 10, 2021, https://vimeo.com/517515536.

2. James Baldwin, *Notes of a Native Son* (Boston: Beacon, 2012), 103.

3. Takudzwa Hillary Chiwanza, "Poverty and Inequality—the Long-Lasting Effect of Apartheid in South Africa," The African Exponent, April 8, 2018, https://www.africanexponent.com/post/8927-south-africa-is-one-of-the-most-unequal-countries-in-the-world.

4. Victor Sulla and Precious Zikhali, "Overcoming Poverty and Inequality in South Africa: An Assessment of Drivers, Constraints and Opportunities, March 22, 2018, http://documents.worldbank.org/curated/en/530481521735906534/Overcoming-Poverty-and-Inequality-in-South-Africa-An-Assessment-of-Drivers-Constraints-and-Opportunities.

5. The World Bank in South Africa, "Key Development Challenges," accessed October 6, 2021, https://www.worldbank.org/en/country/southafrica/overview#1.

6. Rudy Wiebe and Yvonne Johnson, *Stolen Life: The Journey of a Cree Woman* (Toronto: Jackpine House, 1998).

7. Brené Brown, "Shame v. Guilt," *Brené Brown* (blog), January 14, 2013, https://brenebrown.com/blog/2013/01/14/shame-v-guilt.

8. Brown, "Shame v. Guilt."

9. Mannette Morgan, *Finding Your Voice: A Path to Recovery for Survivors of Abuse* (Issaquah, WA: Made for Success, 2019), 219.

10. Thomas Norman DeWolf and Jodie Geddes, *The Little Book of Racial Healing* (New York: Good Books, 2019), 6.

11. Erwin Raphael McManus, *The Artisan Soul* (New York: HarperCollins, 2014), 168.

Chapter 6 The Liberating Jesus

1. Hafiz, *The Gift: Poems by Hafiz*, trans. Daniel Landisky (New York: Penguin Compass, 1999), 141.

2. Angeles Arrien, *Signs of Life: The Five Universal Shapes and How to Use Them* (New York: Tarcher/Putnam, 1992), 39.

3. Isabel Wilkerson, *Caste: The Origins of Our Discontents* (New York: Random House, 2020), 6.

4. John Blake, "This Is What 'Whitelash' Looks Like," CNN, November 19, 2016, https://www.cnn.com/2016/11/11/us/obama-trump-white-backlash/index.html.

5. *Cambridge Dictionary*, s.v. "Whitelash," accessed September 9, 2021, https://dictionary.cambridge.org/dictionary/english/whitelash.

6. Resmaa Menakem, *My Grandmother's Hands: Racialized Trauma and the Pathway to Mending Our Hearts and Bodies* (Las Vegas: Central Recovery, 2017), 28.

Chapter 7 The Heart of a Learner

1. *Intotemak*, Special Issue (Fall/Winter 2016), inside front cover.

2. Eric Hoffer, *Reflections on the Human Condition* (Titusville: Hopewell, 2006), 26.

3. Lexico, s.v. "colonization," accessed March 28, 2021, https://www.lexico.com/definition/colonization.

4. Richard Wagamese, *One Drum: Stories and Ceremonies for a Planet* (Madeira Park: Douglas and McIntyre, 2019), 91.

5. Kaitlin Curtice (@kaitlincurtice), "The heart space that an ally should inhabit: There is so much I don't know. I want to learn more. I am ready to listen before speaking. There is so much I don't know," Twitter, July 6, 2018, 12:15 p.m., https://twitter.com/KaitlinCurtice/status/1015267952776630272. Used with permission.

Chapter 8 Mutuality

1. Richard Wagamese, *Embers: One Ojibway's Meditations* (Madeira Park, BC: Douglas and McIntyre, 2013), 36.

2. Antoinette Sithole, "Truth and Reconciliation Commission Human Rights Violations—Questions and Answers," July 22, 1996, https://www.justice.gov.za/trc/hrvtrans/soweto/sithole.htm.

3. Sandiswa L. Kobe, "Ubuntu as a Spirituality of Liberation for Black Theology of Liberation," *HTS Teologiese Studies / Theological Studies* 77, no. 3 (January 2021): 3, https://doi.org/10.4102/hts.v77i3.6176.

4. Desmond M. Tutu, *No Future without Forgiveness* (London: Rider, 1999), 5.

5. Tutu, *No Future without Forgiveness*, 6.

6. Martin Luther King Jr., "Letter from a Birmingham Jail," African Studies Center, University of Pennsylvania, April 16, 1963, https://www.africa.upenn.edu/Articles_Gen/Letter_Birmingham.html.

7. History.com Editors, "Trail of Tears," History, November 9, 2009, https://www.history.com/topics/native-american-history/trail-of-tears.

8. Abraham Joshua Heschel, *Moral Grandeur and Spiritual Audacity* (New York: Farrar, Strauss & Giroux, 1996), loc. 4793 of 8973, Kindle.

9. Heschel, *Moral Grandeur and Spiritual Audacity*, loc. 431 of 8973.

10. Mungi Ngomane, *Everyday Ubuntu: Living Better Together, the African Way* (Vancouver: Appetite by Random House, 2020), 14.

11. Tutu, *No Freedom without Forgiveness*, 34–35.

12. Ngomane, *Everyday Ubuntu*, 13.

13. Sophie B. Oluwole, "African Philosophers You May Not Have Heard Of," *Flow*, October/November 2018, 129.

Part 3 Repent

1. Kris Rocke and Joel Van Dyke, *Geography of Grace: Doing Theology from Below* (Tacoma: Street Psalms Press, 2012), loc. 1249 of 4889, Kindle.

Chapter 9 Repentance

1. Anneliese A. Singh, *The Racial Healing Handbook* (Oakland: New Harbinger, 2019), 173.

2. Brown, *I'm Still Here*, 107.

3. Brown, *I'm Still Here*, 108.

4. Brown, *I'm Still Here*, 109–10.

5. "Oxford Union Debate (December 3, 1964)," *Malcolm X* (blog), accessed August 24, 2021, http://malcolmxfiles.blogspot.com/2013/07/oxford-union-debate-december-3-1964.html.

6. "The National Memorial for Peace and Justice," Equal Justice Institute, accessed May 15, 2021, https://museumandmemorial.eji.org/.

7. Equal Justice Initiative, "Community Remembrance Project Catalogue: A New Commitment to Truth and Justice," https://simplebooklet.com/crpcatalog, 147, 137.

8. Equal Justice Initiative, "Community Remembrance Project Catalogue," 147.

9. "Resmaa Menakem: Notice the Rage; Notice the Silence," *On Being* with Krista Tippett, June 4, 2020, https://onbeing.org/programs/resmaa-menakem-notice-the-rage-notice-the-silence.

10. Latasha Morrison, *Be the Bridge: Pursuing God's Heart for Racial Reconciliation* (Colorado Springs: Waterbrook, 2019), 146.

11. Soong-Chan Rah, Mae Elise Cannon, Lisa Sharon Harper, and Troy Jackson, *Forgive Us: Confessions of a Compromised Faith* (Grand Rapids: Zondervan, 2014), 18.

12. Kaitlin Curtice, *Native: Identity, Belonging, and Rediscovering God* (Grand Rapids: Brazos, 2020), 105.

13. Layla F. Saad, *Me and White Supremacy* (Naperville, IL: Sourcebooks, 2020), 3.

Chapter 10 Seeking Justice

1. "About," Lilla: International Women's Network, accessed May 15, 2021, https://lillanetwork.wordpress.com/about/.

2. Leon Wessels, *Vereeniging, Die Onvoltooide Vrede* (Kaapstad: Umuzi, 2010), 12.

3. To read more about these Batwa families, see Kelley Nikondeha, *Adopted: The Sacrament of Belonging in a Fractured World* (Grand Rapids: Eerdmans, 2017).

4. "The Situation of the Batwa Indigenous Peoples in Burundi," Indigenous Peoples Major Group for Sustainable Development, accessed October 6, 2021, https://indigenouspeoples-sdg.org/index.php/english/ttt/1037-the-situation-of -the-batwa-indigenous-peoples-in-burundi.

5. You can read about this in Idelette McVicker, "Can Love Move This Mountain?," *SheLoves Magazine*, January 31, 2012, https://shelovesmagazine.com/2012 /sheloves-bubanza-project-can-love-move-this-mountain-in-burundi/.

6. You can read more of this story in Idelette McVicker, "We Danced on Holy Ground," *SheLoves Magazine*, June 12, 2012, https://shelovesmagazine.com/2012 /bubanza-we-danced-on-holy-ground/.

7. Walter Brueggemann, "Scriptural Authority in the Post-Critical Period," in *The Anchor Bible Dictionary*, ed. David Noel Freedman (New York: Doubleday, 1992), 5:1054–55.

8. Nicole Joshua, email message to author with attachment, September 13, 2017.

9. "To Be in a Rage, Almost All the Time," NPR, June 1, 2020, https://www .npr.org/2020/06/01/867153918/-to-be-in-a-rage-almost-all-the-time.

10. USF Urban Education & Social Justice, "Color of Fear—What It Means to Be American," YouTube, September 11, 2013, https://www.youtube.com /watch?v=2nmhAJYxFT4.

11. "Thich Nhat Hanh on Compassionate Listening, SuperSoul Sunday, Oprah Winfrey Network," YouTube, May 6, 2012, https://www.youtube.com /watch?v=lyUxYflkhzo.

12. "I Walk in the History of My People," *This Bridge Called My Back: Writings by Radical Women of Color*, 4th ed., ed. Cherrie Moraga and Gloria Anzaldúa (Albany: State University of New York Press, 2015), 53.

13. This quotation is explained on *Inward/Outward Together* in this man-ner: "[This quotation] is often attributed to the Talmud, but is more accurately described as a loose translation of commentary on a portion of the *Pirke Avot*, which is itself a commentary on Micah 6:8. See *Wisdom of the Jewish Sages: A Modern Reading of* Pirke Avot by Rabbi Rami Shapiro." "Do Not Be Daunted," *Inward/Outward Together* (blog), December 7, 2020, https://inwardoutward.org /do-not-be-daunted-dec-7-2020.

14. Nicole A. Cardoza, "Study Hall: How Do I Address White Saviorism?," *Anti-Racism Daily*, August 28, 2021, https://ckarchive.com/b/o8ukhqh2xnr0.

Part 4 Recalibrate

1. "From 'The Telly Cycle' by Toi Derricotte," Rattle.com, October 28, 2014, https://www.rattle.com/from-the-telly-cycle-by-toi-derricotte/.

2. Steven Charleston, *Ladder to the Light: An Indigenous Elder's Meditations on Hope and Courage* (Minneapolis: Broadleaf, 2021), 26.

Chapter 11 The Way of Relationship

1. Paulo Freire, *Pedagogy of the Oppressed* (London: Penguin, 1996), 114.

2. "Chief Dr. Robert Joseph, O.B.C., O.C.," Reconciliation Canada, March 12, 2021, https://reconciliationcanada.ca/about/team/chief-dr-robert-joseph/. Chief Dr. Robert Joseph is hereditary chief of the Gwawaenuk First Nation and an ambassador for Reconciliation Canada.

3. Hermann Giliomee, *Die Afrikaners: 'n Biografie* (Kaapstad: Tafelberg, 2004), 120–53.

4. For more understanding about the complexity of Afrikaans as language—both as a language of the oppressor and as a language of liberation, you can check out "Afrikaans: The Language of Black and Coloured Dissent," South African History Online, March 30, 2021, https://www.sahistory.org.za/article/afrikaans-language-black-and-coloured-dissent.

5. I so appreciate the work of Mickey ScottBey Jones on the idea of brave space and not just safe space. See Mickey ScottBey Jones, "Invitation to Brave Space," accessed March 30, 2021, https://onbeing.org/poetry/invitation-to-brave-space/.

6. Richard Fausset, Neil Vigdor, and Giulia McDonnell Nieto del Rio, "8 Dead in Atlanta Spa Shootings, with Fears of Anti-Asian Bias," *New York Times*, March 26, 2021, https://www.nytimes.com/live/2021/03/17/us/shooting-atlanta-acworth.

7. Scott Glover, Collette Richards, Curt Devine, and Drew Griffin, "A Key Miscalculation by Officers Contributed to the Tragic Death of Breonna Taylor," CNN, July 23, 2020, https://www.cnn.com/2020/07/23/us/breonna-taylor-police-shooting-invs/index.html.

8. *The Next Question*, "Ep 6: Brave Together," Vimeo, accessed May 15, 2021, https://vimeo.com/371303441.

9. *The Color of Fear (Part Two)*, StirFry Seminars & Consulting Diversity Training Films, March 30, 2021, https://www.diversitytrainingfilms.com/films-2/the-color-of-fear-2-walking-each-other-home/.

10. Otegha Uwagba, *Whites: On Race and Other Falsehoods* (London: 4th Estate, 2020), 35.

11. Uwagba, *Whites*, 35.

12. Resmaa Menakem, "What Somatic Abolition Is," accessed August 22, 2021, https://www.resmaa.com/movement.

13. Menakem, "What Somatic Abolition Is."

14. Menakem, "What Somatic Abolition Is."

Chapter 12 Honoring Everyone

1. Donna Hicks, *Dignity: The Essential Role It Plays in Resolving Conflict* (New Haven: Yale University Press, 2011), 3–4.

2. Miroslav Volf, "All Due Respect: Honoring Others," *Christian Century*, August 1, 2011, https://www.christiancentury.org/article/2011-07/all-due-respect.

3. Trigger warning: this video contains racist rhetoric. DocsOnline, "Eugene Terre'Blanche's Afrikaner Resistance Movement—Rally," YouTube, March 28, 2011, https://www.youtube.com/watch?v=QbvzZTB9O0k.

4. Debbie Ford, *The Dark Side of the Light Chasers* (New York: Riverhead, 2010), 5.

5. Ford, *Dark Side of the Light Chasers*, 5.

6. Ford, *Dark Side of the Light Chasers*, 73.

7. Ford, *Dark Side of the Light Chasers*, 68.

8. Ashlee Eiland, *Human (Kind): How Reclaiming Human Worth and Embracing Radical Kindness Will Bring Us Back Together* (Colorado Springs: Waterbrook, 2020), 4.

9. Robin Wall Kimmerer, *Braiding Sweetgrass: Indigenous Wisdom, Scientific Knowledge, and the Teachings of Plants* (Minneapolis: Milkweed, 2013), 195.

Chapter 13 Knitted Together

1. "The Powerful Lesson Maya Angelou Taught Oprah," OWN, aired October 19, 2011, https://www.oprah.com/oprahs-lifeclass/the-powerful-lesson-maya-angelou-taught-oprah-video.

2. Michael Lapsley and Stephen Karakashian, *Redeeming the Past* (Maryknoll, NY: Orbis Books, 2012), 4.

3. Institute for Healing of Memories, https://www.healing-memories.org.

4. Lapsley and Karakashian, *Redeeming the Past*, 243–45.

5. "Dr. Rachel Naomi Remen: The Difference between Curing and Healing," *On Being* with Krista Tippett, August 11, 2005, https://onbeing.org/programs/rachel-naomi-remen-the-difference-between-fixing-and-healing-nov2018/.

6. "Dr. Rachel Naomi Remen."

7. "Dr. Rachel Naomi Remen."

8. "Dr. Rachel Naomi Remen."

9. Lucinda Dordley, "Why Cape Town Is Called the 'Mother City' . . . ," Cape Town Etc, March 15, 2018, https://www.capetownetc.com/cape-town/cape-town-called-mother-city/.

10. Alia Chughtai, "Know Their Names: Black People Killed by the Police in the US," Al Jazeera, accessed March 29, 2021, https://interactive.aljazeera.com/aje/2020/know-their-names/index.html.

11. Kelley Nikondeha, *Adopted: The Sacrament of Belonging* (Grand Rapids: Eerdmans, 2017), 112.

Chapter 14 Contending for Peace

1. "Mother Teresa Reflects on Working toward Peace," Santa Clara University, accessed August 22, 2021, https://www.scu.edu/mcae/architects-of-peace/Teresa/essay.html.

2. Learn more about the Global Immersion Project in the book by the founders: Jon Huckins and Jer Swigart, *Mending the Divides: Creative Love in a Conflicted World* (Downers Grove, IL: IVP, 2017).

3. Ayelet Waldman, "The Shame of Shuhada Street Hebron," *The Atlantic*, June 12, 2014, https://www.theatlantic.com/international/archive/2014/06/the-shame-of-shuhada-street-hebron/372639/.

4. "Jimmy Carter Defends 'Peace Not Apartheid,'" NPR, January 25, 2007, https://www.npr.org/templates/story/story.php?storyId=7004473.

5. "Apartheid Legislation 1850s–1970s," South African History Online, accessed March 29, 2021, https://www.sahistory.org.za/article/apartheid-legislation-1850s-1970s.

6. Jaime Black, "The REDress Project," accessed March 29, 2021, https://www.jaimeblackartist.com/exhibitions/.

7. "Reclaiming Power and Place: The Final Report of the National Inquiry into Missing and Murdered Indigenous Women and Girls," National Inquiry into Missing and Murdered Indigenous Women and Girls, accessed March 29, 2021, https://www.mmiwg-ffada.ca/final-report/.

8. "About PCFF," The Parents Circle–Families Forum, accessed March 29, 2021, https://www.theparentscircle.org/en/about_eng/.

9. Moira's story appears here: "Moira Jilani—'I Came Back to Palestine and Lost Ziad,'" The Parents Circle–Families Forum, accessed March 29, 2021, https://www.theparentscircle.org/en/stories/moira-jilani_eng/.

10. Rami's story appears here: "Rami Elhanan—'Replacing Pain with Hope,'" The Parents Circle—Families Forum, accessed March 29, 2021, https://www.theparentscircle.org/en/stories/rami-elhanan_eng/.

11. "About Holy Land Trust," Holy Land Trust, accessed May 15, 2021, https://www.holylandtrust.org/about.

12. "The People of Other Voice," Other Voice, accessed March 29, 2021, http://www.othervoice.org/info/info-006.htm.

13. Roald Høvring, "Gaza: The World's Largest Open-Air Prison," Norwegian Refugee Council, April 26, 2018, https://www.nrc.no/news/2018/april/gaza-the-worlds-largest-open-air-prison/.

14. Kamel Hawwash, "Where Is Gaza Heading in 2020?," Arab Weekly, January 5, 2020, https://thearabweekly.com/where-gaza-heading-2020.

15. "Stop Decorating the 'Wall of Shame,'" The Observers, last modified October 6, 2010, https://observers.france24.com/en/20091021-stop-decorating-wall-shame-israel-palestine-seperation-graffiti.

16. Eli Laslow, Rising Out of Hatred: The Awakening of a Former White Nationalist (Toronto: Doubleday, 2018), 29.

17. Laslow, Rising Out of Hatred, 48–49.

18. Laslow, Rising Out of Hatred, 80.

19. Laslow, Rising Out of Hatred, 81.

20. "LGBTQ2S+: What Does It Mean?," Kids Help Phone, June 19, 2018, https://kidshelpphone.ca/get-info/lgbtq2s-what-does-it-mean.

21. Lisa Sharon Harper, The Very Good Gospel: How Everything Wrong Can Be Made Right (Colorado Springs: WaterBrook, 2016), 13.

22. Erica Glover, "Live Like Mother Teresa: Finding Your Own Calcutta," Franciscan Media, March 13, 2018, https://www.franciscanmedia.org/franciscan-spirit-blog/live-like-mother-teresa-finding-your-own-calcutta.

Chapter 15 Listening for the Truth-Tellers

1. Austin Channing Brown, I'm Still Here: Black Dignity in a World Made for Whiteness (New York: Convergent, 2018), 117.

2. Kairos Blanket Exercise Community, https://www.kairosblanketexercise.org.

3. The Global Immersion Project, https://globalimmerse.org.

4. Tanya Talaga, *Seven Fallen Feathers: Racism, Death, and Hard Truths in a Northern City* (Toronto: Anansi, 2017), 58–64.

5. A term used by Duncan Campbell Scott, who might be called an extreme assimilationist. "Until There Is Not a Single Indian in Canada," Facing History and Ourselves, accessed March 30, 2021, https://www.facinghistory.org/stolen -lives-indigenous-peoples-canada-and-indian-residential-schools/historical-back ground/until-there-not-single-indian-canada.

6. Pierre Bélanger and Kate Yoon, "Canada's Apartheid," Lapsus Lima, November 27, 2018, https://www.lapsuslima.com/canadas-apartheid/.

7. Bélanger and Yoon, "Canada's Apartheid."

8. Talaga, *Seven Fallen Feathers*, 58.

9. Talaga, *Seven Fallen Feathers*, 59.

10. Bélanger and Yoon, "Canada's Apartheid."

11. Thomas Berger, "The BC Indian Land Question and the Rights of the Indian People" (speech to the Ninth Annual Convention of the Nishga Tribal Council, Port Edwards, B.C., November 1, 1966), 3, in Daniel Raunet's *Without Surrender, without Consent: A History of the Nishga Land Claims* (Toronto: Douglas and McIntyre, 1984), 167.

12. Michaëlle Jean, "Speaking the Truth for a New Beginning," *Michaëlle Jean* (blog), June 30, 2020, https://www.michaellejean.ca/news-actualites/2020 -6-30/speakingnbspthe-truthnbspfornbspanbspnew-beginning.

13. "Indigenous Peoples in Taiwan," International Work Group for Indigenous Affairs, accessed March 30, 2021, https://www.iwgia.org/en/taiwan.

14. "Residential School History," National Centre for Truth and Reconciliation, accessed March 30, 2021, https://nctr.ca/education/teaching-resources /residential-school-history/; Lloyd Dolha, "The Sixties Scoop: How Canada's 'Best Intentions' Proved Catastrophic," First Nations Drum, March 24, 2009, http://www.firstnationsdrum.com/2009/03/the-sixties-scoop-how-canadas-best -intentions-proved-catastrophic/; "Suicide among First Nations People, Métis and Inuit (2011–2016): Findings from the 2011 Canadian Census Health and Environment Cohort (CanCHEC)," Statistics Canada, June 28, 2019, https:// www150.statcan.gc.ca/n1/en/catalogue/99-011-X2019001; Greg Macdougall, "Canada's Indigenous Suicide Crisis Is Worse Than We Thought," Canada's National Observer, September 10, 2019, https://www.nationalobserver.com/2019 /09/10/analysis/canadas-indigenous-suicide-crisis-worse-we-thought; Corinna Dally-Starna, "Water Crisis in First Nations Communities Runs Deeper Than Long-Term Drinking Water Advisories," The Conversation, November 26, 2020, https://theconversation.com/water-crisis-in-first-nations-communities-runs -deeper-than-long-term-drinking-water-advisories-148977; and "Reclaiming Power and Place: The Final Report of the National Inquiry into Missing and Murdered Indigenous Women and Girls," National Inquiry into Missing and Murdered Indigenous Women and Girls, accessed March 29, 2021, https://www .mmiwg-ffada.ca/final-report/.

15. "Canada: 182 Unmarked Graves Found at Another Residential School," Aljazeera, Jun 30, 2021, https://www.aljazeera.com/news/2021/6/30/canada-182 -unmarked-graves-found-at-another-residential-school.

16. "Territory Acknowledgement," Native-land.ca, accessed October 6, 2021, https://native-land.ca/resources/territory-acknowledgement/.

17. Kaitlin Curtice, *Native: Identity, Belonging, and Rediscovering God* (Grand Rapids: Brazos, 2020), 109.

18. "I Am Indigenous," CBC News, accessed March 30, 2021, https://www.cbc.ca/news2/interactives/i-am-indigenous-2017/.

Chapter 16 Decolonizing

1. Mark Charles and Soong-Chan Rah, *Unsettling Truths: The Ongoing Dehumanizing Legacy of the Doctrine of Discovery* (Downers Grove: IVP, 2019), 13.

2. Lin-Manuel Miranda, *Hamilton: The Revolution* (New York: Grand Central, 2016), 94.

3. Tina Curiel-Allen, "What Decolonization Is, and What It Means to Me," *TeenVogue*, March 3, 2018, https://www.teenvogue.com/story/what-decolonization-is-and-what-it-means-to-me.

4. "Why Did Western Europe Dominate the Globe?," Cal Tech, September 1, 2015, https://www.caltech.edu/about/news/why-did-western-europe-dominate-globe-47696.

5. For a decolonized history of South Africa, I highly recommend the work of Patric Tariq Mellet, *The Lie of 1652: A Decolonised History of Land* (Cape Town: Tafelberg, 2020).

6. SheLoves Church, "SheLoves Church with Rev. Dr. Cheryl Bear," posted December 12, 2020, https://www.youtube.com/watch?v=kynJwi-cHQE. Rev. Dr. Cheryl Bear is an award-winning singer-songwriter and associate professor at Regent College.

7. Michael Hill, "Afrikaners Cling to Day of the Vow Glory," *Baltimore Sun*, December 17, 1993, https://www.baltimoresun.com/news/bs-xpm-1993-12-17-1993351002-story.html.

8. Hermann Giliomee, *Die Afrikaners: 'n Biografie* (Kaapstad: Tafelberg, 2004), 124–25.

9. Luke Daniel, "Reconciliation Day: Revisiting the Battle of Blood River," The South African, December 16, 2019, https://www.thesouthafrican.com/opinion/day-of-reconciliation-battle-of-blood-river/.

10. Please see the extensive work on the shaping of dysfunctional theology and the narrative of exceptionalism in the United States by Mark Charles and Soong-Chan Rah, *Unsettling Truths: The Ongoing Dehumanizing Legacy of the Doctrine of Discovery* (Downers Grove: IVP, 2019), 69–116.

11. Jon Schwarz, "As Teddy Roosevelt's Statue Falls, Let's Remember How Truly Dark His History Was," The Intercept, June 22, 2020, https://theintercept.com/2020/06/22/as-teddy-roosevelts-statue-falls-lets-remember-how-truly-dark-his-history-was/.

12. Artist and activist Andre Henry highlighted the story of Stone Mountain, Georgia, when he was a guest on *The Next Question*. See "Ep 2: Power to the People (Andre Henry)," YouTube, October 13, 2019, https://www.youtube.com/watch?v=dW5nfPkP0hI.

13. Zubeida Jaffer, "Googling 'Jan van Riebeeck'? This Is for You," Africa Is a Country, June 4, 2015, https://africasacountry.com/2015/04/the-eight-years-of-jan-van-riebeeck.

Chapter 17 Re-membering

1. Kaitlin Curtice, *Native: Identity, Belonging, and Rediscovering God* (Grand Rapids: Brazos, 2020), 108.

2. "District Six Is Declared a 'White Area,'" South African History Online, February 8, 2016, https://www.sahistory.org.za/article/district-six-declared-white-area.

3. "District Six," Cape Town History, accessed March 30, 2021, http://cape townhistory.com/?page_id=238.

4. District Six Museum, https://www.districtsix.co.za.

5. "Missing and Murdered Aboriginal Women: A National Operational Overview," Royal Canadian Mounted Police, accessed March 30, 2021, https://www.rcmp-grc.gc.ca/en/missing-and-murdered-aboriginal-women-national-operational-overview.

6. "Reclaiming Power and Place: The Final Report of the National Inquiry into Missing and Murdered Indigenous Women and Girls," National Inquiry into Missing and Murdered Indigenous Girls, accessed October 7, 2021, https://www.mmiwg-ffada.ca/.

7. "Reclaiming Power and Place."

8. "Genocide of Indigenous Peoples," Holocaust Museum Houston, accessed March 20, 2021, https://hmh.org/library/research/genocide-of-indigenous-peoples-guide/.

9. "Welcome to Zatoun," Zatoun, https://zatoun.com/.

10. "Trees for Life Sponsorship," Zatoun, https://zatoun.com/product/trees-for-life/.

Chapter 18 Practicing Restitution

1. Ta-Nehisi Coates, "The Case for Reparations," *The Atlantic*, June 2014, https://www.theatlantic.com/magazine/archive/2014/06/the-case-for-reparations/361631/.

2. Jemar Tisby, *The Color of Compromise* (Grand Rapids: Zondervan, 2019), 197.

3. An adaptation of a story told in Sharlene Swartz, *Another Country: Everyday Social Restitution* (Cape Town: BestRed, 2016), xxv; and Michael Lapsley and Stephen Karakashian, *Redeeming the Past* (Maryknoll, NY: Orbis Books, 2012), 152.

4. "Questions," Restitution Foundation, March 23, 2021, https://www.restitu tion.org.za/questions/.

5. Lapsley and Karakashian, *Redeeming the Past*, 152. Please note: In the ebook version, the quotation is as above. In the printed version the sentence reads as follows: "Forgiveness and healing relationships involve making restitution for what has been stolen. I have to return the bike." I am referencing the print version but quoting the ebook version.

6. Liam Knox, "New Study Shows Racism May Shorten Black Americans' Lifespans," NBC News, February 5, 2020, https://www.nbcnews.com/news/nbcblk/new-study-shows-racism-may-shorten-black-americans-lifespans-n1128351.

7. Ruth Messinger, "2009 Baccalaureate Remarks by Ruth Messinger," *Stanford Report*, June 17, 2009, https://news.stanford.edu/news/2009/june17/messinger_text-061709.html.

8. The Restitution Foundation, accessed March 23, 2021, https://www.restitution.org.za/. To find this quotation, click through the banner with photos of the team until you come to Marlyn Faure.

9. Coates, "Case for Reparations."

10. Swartz, *Another Country*, xxvii.

11. Amy-Jill Levine, *Light of the World: A Beginner's Guide to Advent* (Nashville: Abingdon, 2019), 31.

12. Levine, *Light of the World*, 75.

13. Swartz, *Another Country*, xiii.

14. Lapsley and Karakashian, *Redeeming the Past*, 151.

15. Lapsley and Karakashian, *Redeeming the Past*, 149.

16. Lapsley and Karakashian, *Redeeming the Past*, 151.

17. Swartz, *Another Country*, xxix.

Chapter 19 Using Power for Good

1. Mary Dana Hinton, "Deeper Understanding for People of Good Will," Hollins University, YouTube, January 18, 2021, https://www.youtube.com/watch?v=t2-7oJpbw78.

2. Gloria Steinem, *My Life on the Road* (New York: Random House, 2016), 22.

3. Cedar Barstow and Reynold Ruslan Feldman, *Living in the Power Zone: How Right Use of Power Can Transform Relationships* (Boulder: Many Realms, 2013), 19.

4. Martin Luther King Jr., *Where Do We Go From Here: Chaos or Community?* (Boston: Beacon, 2010), 38.

5. Dr. Chanequa Walker-Barnes, "Pathological Whiteness: Diagnosing the Hidden Wound," TheoEd Talks, Vimeo, March 10, 2021, https://vimeo.com/517515536.

6. Mark Braverman, *A Wall in Jerusalem* (Nashville: Jericho, 2013), 133.

7. Clarissa Pinkola Estés, "You Were Made for This," Awakin, March 29, 2021, https://www.awakin.org/read/view.php?tid=548.

8. Beverly Daniel Tatum, *Why Are All the Black Kids Sitting Together in the Cafeteria?*, 3rd ed. (New York: Basic Books, 2017), 161.

Chapter 20 Reclaiming Our Humanity

1. Harriet Beecher Stowe, "Sojourner Truth the Libyan Sibyl," *The Atlantic*, April 1863, https://www.theatlantic.com/magazine/archive/1863/04/sojourner-truth-the-libyan-sibyl/308775/.

2. Richard Rohr, "The Path of Descent: Participating in God," Center for Action and Contemplation, August 2, 2017, https://cac.org/participating-in-god-2017-08-02/.

3. Willie James Jennings, *The Christian Imagination: Theology and the Origins of Race* (New Haven: Yale University Press, 2010), 15.

4. Soong-Chan Rah, Mae Elise Cannon, Lisa Sharon Harper, and Troy Jackson, *Forgive Us: Confessions of a Compromised Faith* (Grand Rapids: Zondervan, 2014), 98.

5. Booker T. Washington, *Up from Slavery: An Autobiography*, The Literature Page, accessed March 28, 2021, http://www.literaturepage.com/read/upfromslavery -66.html.

6. Resmaa Menakem, *My Grandmother's Hands: Racialized Trauma and the Pathway to Mending Our Hearts and Bodies* (Las Vegas: Central Recovery, 2017), 147–48.

7. "Life Aboard a Slave Ship," History, March 8, 2021, https://www.history .com/topics/slavery/life-aboard-a-slave-ship-video.

8. Osheta Moore, *Dear White Peacemakers: Dismantling Racism with Grit and Grace* (Harrisonburg, VA: Herald, 2021), 35.

AUTHOR BIO

Idelette McVicker was born and raised in South Africa and later worked as a journalist in Taipei, Taiwan, before moving to Vancouver, Canada. She founded *SheLoves Magazine*, the editorial pillar of SheLoves Media Society, a global community of women committed to freedom, justice, and transformation. Learn more at Idelette.com and SheLovesMagazine.com.